hamlyn cookery club

More than mince

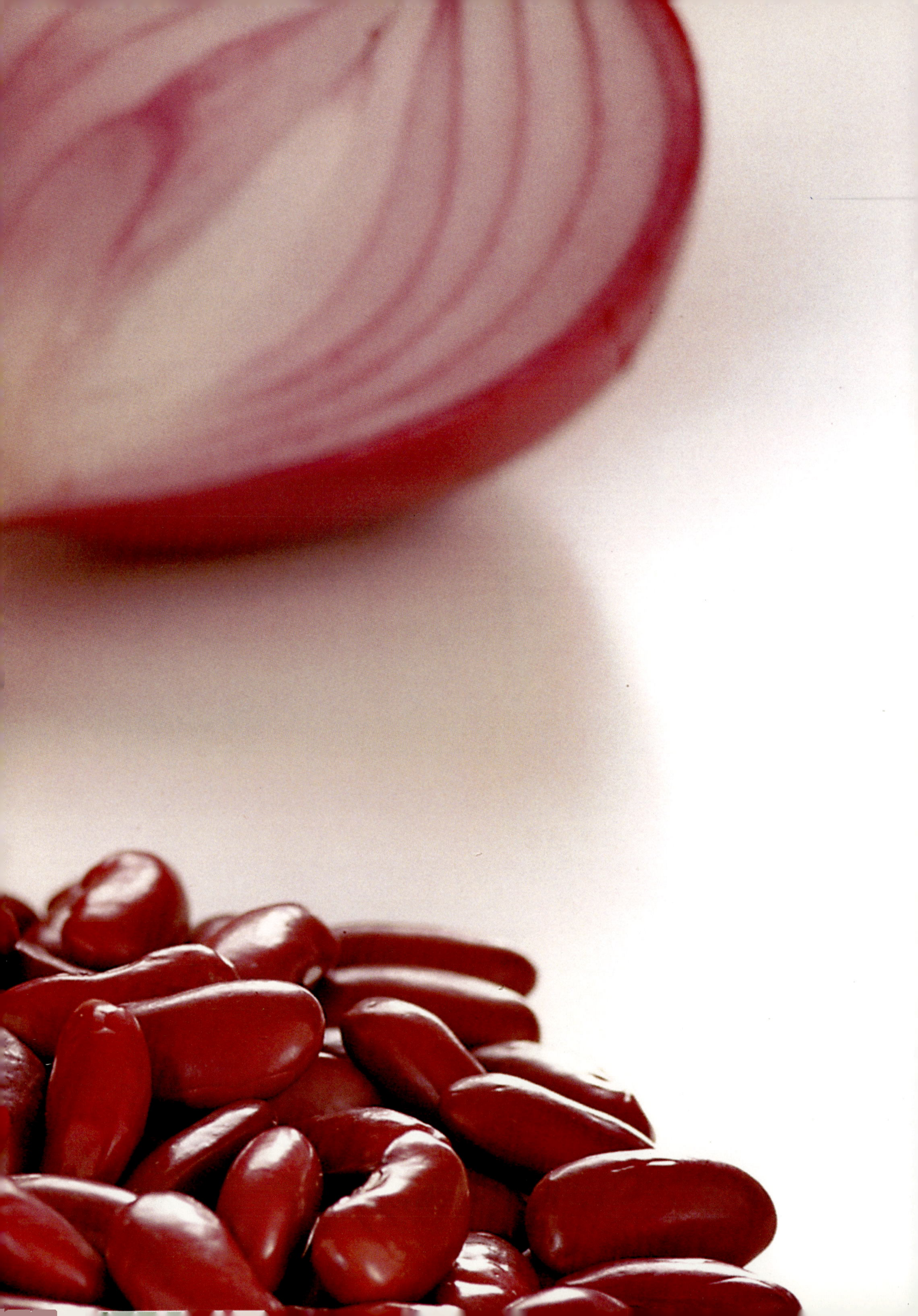

hamlyn cookery club

More than mince

First published in 2000 by Hamlyn
a division of Octopus Publishing Group Ltd
2–4 Heron Quays
London E14 4JP

Reprinted 2001

Copyright © 2000 Octopus Publishing Group Ltd
All Photography Copyright © 2000 Octopus Publishing Group Ltd

All rights reserved. No part of this publication may be reproduced, stored in a retrieval system, or transmitted, in any form or by any means, electronic, electrostatic, magnetic tape, mechanical, photocopying, recording or otherwise without the prior written permission of the publisher.

British Library Cataloguing-in-Publication Data
A catalogue record for this book is available from the British Library.

ISBN 0 600 59991 4

Printed in China

Copy Editor: Heather Thomas
Creative Director: Keith Martin
Design Manager: Bryan Dunn
Designer: Ginny Zeal
Jacket Photography: Sean Myers
Picture Researcher: Christine Junemann
Senior Production Controller: Katherine Hockley

Notes

1 Both metric and imperial measurements have been given in all recipes. Use one set of measurements only and not a mixture of both.

2 Standard level spoon measurements are used in all recipes.
1 tablespoon = one 15 ml spoon
1 teaspoon = one 5 ml spoon

3 Eggs should be medium unless otherwise stated. The Department of Health advises that eggs should not be consumed raw. This book may contain dishes made with raw or lightly cooked eggs. It is prudent for more vulnerable people such as pregnant or nursing mothers, the elderly, babies and young children to avoid these dishes. Once prepared, these dishes should be refrigerated and eaten promptly.

4 Milk should be full fat unless otherwise stated.

5 Fresh herbs should be used unless otherwise stated. If unavailable use dried herbs as an alternative but halve the quantities stated.

6 Pepper should be freshly ground black pepper unless otherwise stated.

7 Ovens should be preheated to the specified temperature – if using a fan-assisted oven, follow the manufacturer's instructions for adjusting the time and temperature.

8 Measurements for canned food have been given as a standard metric equivalent.

Contents

Introduction 6

Starters and Snacks 8

Pasta and Rice 24

Pastry, Pizza and Pancakes 40

Burgers, Meatballs and Meat Loaves 50

Baked in the Oven 74

Index 96

Introduction

Economical and highly nutritious, mince is wonderfully versatile and can be used as the main ingredient in a wide range of dishes, from pâtés and pasta sauces to hamburgers, kebabs, meatballs and meat loaves. Mince is a cheap form of protein and a little can be padded out with vegetables, pasta or rice to make a more substantial meal.

TYPES OF MINCE
You can buy ready-minced meat or mince it yourself at home. Many types of mince tend to be quite high in fat so, for the sake of your health, it is usually better to choose extra lean mince, even though you will have to pay a little more for it.
- **Minced beef:** this is the basis for most hamburgers, meat loaves and classic pasta sauces. Minced steak or extra lean minced beef are the most healthy choices.
- **Minced chicken and turkey:** these are very low in fat and great for making into burgers and meatballs.
- **Minced lamb:** any boneless lean cuts of lamb are suitable for mincing. Minced lamb is very popular in Middle Eastern dishes. It is often flavoured with aromatic spices and made into meatballs and kebabs. It is also the traditional ingredient in shepherd's pie and moussaka.
- **Minced pork:** you can use lean pork or pork belly mince depending on the recipe. Try mixing it with grated onions and fresh herbs to make delicious burgers.
- **Minced veal:** pie veal is suitable for mincing. It is ideal for meat loaves.

EQUIPMENT
If you want to mince the meat yourself, it is best to use an old-fashioned clamp-on mincer or a special mincing attachment to your electric mixer. A food processor can also be used for mincing but the mince will be very finely ground indeed, and more suitable for pâtés. Before mincing meat, trim away and discard any skin, gristle and most of the fat.

BUYING, STORING AND FREEZING MINCE

When buying mince, check that it looks really fresh and is not discoloured. Don't be tempted by reduced-price mince which is on its sell-by date. It is always best to cook mince on the day of purchase as it does not keep well. Otherwise, wrap and store it overnight in the refrigerator before using the following day. Mince freezes successfully and you may find it helpful to buy it in larger quantities than you need and then to pack and seal it in 500 g (1 lb) bags. You can also freeze raw hamburgers and meatballs for cooking at a later date.

COOKING AND FLAVOURING MINCE

It is essential that mince is thoroughly cooked. Because it is so versatile, it can be fried or added to sauces and cooked on the hob, or baked in a pie or made into burgers and kebabs and then grilled or barbecued over hot coals.

You can flavour mince with most herbs (fresh or dried) and spices, tomato purée, soy, tabasco or Worcestershire sauces. Good combinations include:
- Minced beef with thyme, fresh coriander or tomato purée.
- Minced lamb with rosemary, mint, coriander or ground spices, such as cumin, allspice and nutmeg.
- Minced pork with sage, onion and parsley.

MINCING COOKED MEAT

Of course, a good way of using up leftover cooked meat, especially beef, lamb, pork, turkey or chicken from a Sunday roast, is to mince it and convert it into another dish. Many of the recipes in this book can be adapted in this way. Traditionally, shepherd's pie and cottage pie were always made with minced cooked meat to transform the leftovers into a nourishing meal for another day. Cooked meat should always be wrapped or stored in a sealed container in the refrigerator away from uncooked meat, and it should be minced and eaten the following day.

Starters and Snacks

Vietnamese Pork Parcels

These are the Vietnamese equivalent of Chinese spring rolls. Instead of using the usual wrappers made from dough that are deep-fried, these pork parcels utilise lettuce leaves to enclose their filling. The result is much fresher and healthier.

2 tablespoons groundnut or vegetable oil
375 g (12 oz) minced pork
5 cm (2 inch) piece of fresh root ginger, peeled and finely chopped
2 garlic cloves, finely chopped
4 spring onions, finely chopped
200 ml (7 fl oz) fish or chicken stock
2 tablespoons soy sauce
2 teaspoons soft dark brown sugar
125 g (4 oz) cooked peeled prawns, coarsely chopped (defrosted and dried thoroughly, if frozen)
1 teaspoon anchovy extract
½ teaspoon chilli powder, or to taste
salt and pepper

To serve:
1 bunch mint and/or basil leaves
16 crisp lettuce leaves, e.g. lollo rosso

Heat a wok, then add the oil and heat over a moderate heat until hot.

Add the pork, ginger, garlic and spring onions and stir-fry for about 5 minutes or until the meat loses its pink colour.

Add the stock, soy sauce and sugar and stir-fry until the stock is absorbed. Add the prawns, anchovy extract and chilli powder and stir-fry for 1–2 minutes until the prawns are heated through. Add salt and pepper to taste and serve at once.

Guests place a few mint or basil leaves inside each lettuce leaf and then add the pork mixture. The lettuce leaf is rolled up around the filling to make a neat parcel which is eaten with the fingers.

Serves 4

Sweet and Sour Minced Pork

Served in crisp chicory leaves, this spicy minced pork makes an attractive first course for a small dinner party with a delicious oriental theme.

3 dried red chillies
1 tablespoon groundnut or vegetable oil
250 g (8 oz) lean minced pork
1 tablespoon soy sauce
1 tablespoon soft dark brown sugar
2 teaspoons dry sherry or sherry vinegar
½ x 550 g (1 lb 2 oz) jar bean sprout salad in wine vinegar
½ x 200 g (7 oz) packet creamed coconut
3 tablespoons chopped fresh coriander
16 large chicory leaves (about 1 large head chicory)
2 teaspoons sesame oil
salt
parsley, to garnish

Put the dried chillies in a wok and dry-fry over a moderate heat for 2–3 minutes. Pound in a mortar with a pestle or crush with the end of a straight wooden rolling pin.

Heat the oil in the wok until hot. Add the pork and pounded chillies and stir-fry over a moderate heat for about 5 minutes or until the meat loses its pink colour. Add the soy sauce, sugar and sherry or vinegar and stir-fry for 1 minute until well blended with the meat.

Stir in the bean sprout salad with its liquid and bring to the boil. Crumble in the creamed coconut, stir-fry until blended and then lower the heat. Simmer for 10–15 minutes until thickened, stirring frequently. Remove from the heat and stir in the chopped coriander and salt to taste.

Arrange the chicory leaves in a circle on a serving platter. Spoon in the pork mixture, sprinkle with the sesame oil and garnish with parsley.

Serves 4

far left: Vietnamese pork parcels
left: sweet and sour minced pork

Rich Pork Pâté

This is a full-flavoured pâté which can be served with plenty of French bread and a full-bodied red wine to make a satisfying lunch, or as a first course hot, with toast.

500 g (1 lb) pig's liver
50 g (2 oz) butter
1 large onion, finely chopped
3 garlic cloves, crushed
500 g (1 lb) minced pork
1 tablespoon juniper berries, crushed
1 teaspoon paprika
6 tablespoons brandy
salt and pepper

To garnish:
2 bay leaves
whole juniper berries

Chop the liver – it does not have to be fine, but large chunks would not be right in the finished pâté. Melt the butter in a large frying pan and brown the liver quickly all over. It is important to make sure that the liver is well sealed and that it is cooked rapidly so that the flavour is kept in each piece. Remove from the pan and place it in a large bowl. Fry the onion and garlic very briefly to take away their raw taste, then add them, with all the pan juices, to the cooked chopped liver.

Mix the minced pork and juniper berries into the liver mixture, then add the paprika and seasoning to taste – be fairly generous. Stir in the brandy, mixing thoroughly.

Spoon the mixture into an ovenproof dish – a plain round one which holds about 900 ml (1½ pints). Make sure that the dish is not too full or some of the juices could be lost during cooking. Smooth the top, then arrange the bay leaves and whole juniper berries on top.

Cover the top with some cooking foil and then stand the dish in a roasting tin. Pour in enough boiling water to come halfway up the sides of the dish. Bake the pâté in a preheated oven, 160°C (325°F), Gas Mark 3, for about 2 hours.

Remove the pâté dish from the roasting tin, place a plate on top and weight this down to press the pâté. If you do not have a plate that fits snugly just inside the top of the cooking dish, then use a large piece of cooking foil, folded over several times. Leave the weighted pâté to cool, and then chill overnight in the refrigerator.

Serve the pâté straight from the dish with fresh bread or toast. Any leftover pâté can be frozen for up to 6 months but it will keep in the refrigerator for several days.

Serves 8–10

above left: rich pork pâté

Pork Terrine

A terrine always makes a good starter if the main course isn't too substantial. If served with crusty French bread and a crisp salad, it is a perfect lunch or supper dish. Do ensure that it is served chilled – the cooked dish will keep for 3–4 days in the refrigerator.

250 g (8 oz) minced pork
250 g (8 oz) minced veal
1 small onion, chopped
1 tablespoon chopped sage
2 tablespoons chopped parsley
1 garlic clove, crushed
125 g (4 oz) mushrooms, chopped
2 eggs
4 rashers of streaky bacon
2 bay leaves
salt and freshly ground black pepper

Lightly grease a 1.5 litre (2½ pint) ovenproof dish or terrine. Mix together the minced pork, veal, onion, herbs, garlic, mushrooms and plenty of seasoning. Lightly beat the eggs and then mix them into the meat mixture.

Pack the mixture into the greased dish or terrine. Remove the bacon rinds and stretch out the rashers with the blade of a knife. Lay the bacon on top of the meat mixture and top with the bay leaves. Cover the terrine closely with a piece of greased greaseproof paper or a butter paper, and then cover with a lid or a piece of foil.

Place the dish in a roasting tin and pour in water to come halfway up the outside of the dish. Cook the terrine in a preheated oven, 180°C (350°F), Gas Mark 4, for 1½ hours.

Take off the coverings and leave to cool at room temperature. When cool, cover the terrine and chill in the refrigerator. Serve from the dish.

Serves 6–8 as a starter, 4–6 as a lunch or supper dish

Pork and Olive Pâté

4 spring onions, chopped
500 g (1 lb) minced pork
250 g (8 oz) sausagemeat
1 tablespoon chopped sage
12 pimiento-stuffed olives, sliced
4 tablespoons dry cider
salt and freshly ground black pepper
To garnish:
tomato slices
chopped parsley

Grease a 500 g (1 lb) loaf tin. Mix the spring onions, pork, sausagemeat, sage, olives and plenty of seasoning.

Blend the mixture with the cider and pack it into the greased loaf tin. Cook in a preheated oven, 180°C (350°F), Gas Mark 4, for 1¼ hours.

Leave to cool, weighted, in the tin. Turn out on to a serving dish and garnish with tomato slices and chopped parsley. Serve with toast.

Serves 6

Mexican Soup

This hearty winter soup is a meal in itself. The beans and chickpeas need to be soaked overnight.

250 g (8 oz) dried chickpeas
250 g (8 oz) dried red kidney beans
2 tablespoons oil
1 onion, chopped
250 g (8 oz) minced beef
1 green pepper, cored, deseeded and chopped
1 x 425 g (14 oz) can tomatoes
450 ml (¾ pint) beef stock
½ teaspoon chilli powder
pinch of salt
garlic or herb bread, to serve

Put the chickpeas and kidney beans in a bowl and then cover with cold water. Leave to soak overnight.

Heat the oil in a pan and sauté the onion until softened. Add the minced beef and then cook, stirring, until browned. Add the green pepper, tomatoes with their juice, drained chickpeas and kidney beans, beef stock, chilli powder and salt. Bring to the boil and boil for 10 minutes, then cover the pan and simmer for 1 hour.

Cool slightly and then blend in a liquidizer or food processor. Add a little stock or water if the soup is too thick. Reheat gently and serve with hot garlic or herb bread.

Serves 4

Steamed Chinese Dumplings

Any leftover dumplings can be reheated either by gently steaming for 5 minutes or by shallow-frying them in a little oil for 6–7 minutes, turning them over once during cooking.

500 g (1 lb) plain flour
4 teaspoons baking powder
250 ml (8 fl oz) water
Filling:
500 g (1 lb) boneless pork (not too lean), minced
1 tablespoon dry sherry
3 tablespoons soy sauce
2 teaspoons sugar
1 teaspoon salt
1 tablespoon sesame oil
2 teaspoons peeled and finely chopped fresh root ginger
1 teaspoon cornflour
To garnish:
julienne of carrot, spring onion, cucumber and fresh root ginger

Sift the flour and baking powder into a mixing bowl. Add the water, mix well and knead lightly. Cover the bowl with a damp cloth and place a small plate over this, then leave the dough to rise at room temperature for 2 hours.

Mix the minced pork with the sherry, soy sauce, sugar, salt, sesame oil, ginger and cornflour.

Divide the dough in half, place on a lightly floured surface and knead. Shape each half into a long, sausage-like roll, 5 cm (2 inches) in diameter. Use a knife to slice each roll into about 15 rounds. Flatten each round with the palm of your hand, then with a rolling pin, and roll out each piece into a pancake, about 7 cm (3 inches) in diameter.

Place 1 tablespoon of the filling in the centre of each pancake. Gather the sides of the pancake up around the filling to meet at the top, and then twist the top of the pancake to close it tightly.

Place a piece of wet muslin on a rack in a steamer and arrange the dumplings about 1 cm (½ inch) apart on the muslin. Cover and steam vigorously for 20 minutes. Serve hot, garnished with the vegetable julienne.

Makes 30

Spiced Bean Curd with Pork

Most of the dishes from the two eastern Chinese provinces of Szechuan and Hunan rely on Szechuan pepper, a piquant spice which is strong and hot, or gain their characteristic heat when chilli peppers are stir-fried in oil scented with onions, garlic and ginger.

1 tablespoon soy sauce
1 tablespoon Chinese rice wine or dry sherry
½ teaspoon sugar
½ teaspoon sesame seed oil
125 g (4 oz) lean boneless pork, finely minced
¼–½ teaspoon Szechuan peppercorns or ½–1 teaspoon black peppercorns
2.5 cm (1 inch) piece of fresh root ginger, peeled and finely chopped
2 garlic cloves, crushed
2 spring onions, chopped
50 ml (2 fl oz) chicken stock
1 tablespoon brown bean sauce
⅛–¼ teaspoon cayenne pepper
250 g (8 oz) bean curd, rinsed, drained and cut into 1 cm (½ inch) cubes
2 tablespoons cooking oil
1 teaspoon cornflour
1 tablespoon cold chicken stock
1 teaspoon sesame seed oil
salt
sprig of dill, to garnish

above left: steamed Chinese dumplings

Combine the soy sauce, rice wine or sherry, sugar and sesame seed oil in a bowl. Add the minced pork, stir well until all the meat is coated, and then cover the bowl and chill in the refrigerator for 30 minutes.

Cook the peppercorns in a wok or a large frying pan over a medium heat, stirring frequently, for about 5 minutes until lightly browned. Remove from the heat and tip the peppercorns out on to a chopping board. Crush to a fine powder with a rolling pin or the back of a spoon, and then set aside.

To make the sauce, combine the ginger, garlic, spring onions, stock, brown bean sauce, cayenne pepper and salt in a small bowl. Set aside.

To cook the pork and bean curd, heat the oil over a medium heat in a wok or a large frying pan. Add the pork and its marinade and stir-fry for 2–3 minutes until the pork is cooked through. Add the sauce mixture and bean curd, then gently stir-fry for 2–3 minutes. Do not stir too vigorously or the bean curd will break up.

Blend the cornflour and chicken stock in a small bowl, then stir into the pork mixture. Stir-fry until the sauce has thickened and becomes clear. Add the crushed peppercorns and sesame seed oil. Transfer to a serving dish, garnish with dill and serve.

Serves 2 as a main course, 4 as part of a Chinese meal.

Steak Tartare

For this classic dish of raw steak, it is essential to use freshly, finely minced fillet or rump steak. It can be served surrounded by mounds of diced raw vegetables – onions and green and red peppers – and finely chopped gherkins and capers.

500 g (1 lb) fillet or rump steak
3 egg yolks
4 tablespoons oil
2 tablespoons chopped parsley
salt and pepper
To garnish:
crisp lettuce leaves
grated horseradish (optional)

Trim away any fat and mince the steak finely. Mix in the egg yolks, oil, parsley and seasoning. Divide the steak mixture into 4 portions and then shape each one into a round, flat cake.

Arrange on a bed of crisp lettuce leaves and, if liked, add a sprinkling of grated horseradish. Baked jacket potatoes or potato crisps go well with steak tartare.

Serves 4

Tacos

In Spanish, 'tacos' simply means snacks. Tacos are eaten all over North America as a portable meal. Tortillas, soft and warm or crisp-fried, are folded in half-moon shapes around a filling which is usually spiced meat. However, you can buy ready made tacos in most stores if you don't have time to make them.

12–16 flour tortillas
Filling:
250 g (8 oz) lean minced beef
125 g (4 oz) lean minced pork
1 teaspoon chilli seasoning
½ teaspoon ground cumin
½ teaspoon ground coriander
pinch of dried oregano
dash of Tabasco sauce
2 tablespoons cider vinegar
175 ml (6 fl oz) bought Enchilada sauce
75 ml (3 fl oz) vegetable oil
To garnish:
125 g (4 oz) grated Cheddar cheese
125 g (4 oz) crisp lettuce, shredded
1 large tomato, coarsely chopped
spring onions, shredded lengthways

Mix the meats and seasonings in a wide, heavy, ungreased frying pan and cook, stirring, over high heat until the meat browns. Add the vinegar and Enchilada sauce and cook for about 10 minutes. If it looks greasy, cool quickly and skim off the fat, then reheat.

For soft tacos, sprinkle the tortillas lightly with cold water, stack, wrap in foil and put on the top shelf of a preheated oven, 140°C (275°F), Gas Mark 1, for 15 minutes.

For crisp tacos, heat 1 cm (½ inch) of vegetable oil in a heavy, deep frying pan. Quickly fry the tortillas, one by one, for about 30 seconds each until they soften. Remove and fold in half. Drop back into the hot oil, holding the edges slightly apart with spaghetti tongs or a fork, and fry quickly on each side for about 30 seconds until crisp. As they cook, stack them on a plate, covered with kitchen paper, in the preheated oven.

Spoon the meat filling into the soft or crisp tortillas, add the garnishes of your choice to taste, and serve the tacos immediately.

Serves 4–6

Meatball Minestrone

2 tablespoons olive oil
2 onions, chopped
4 rashers of rindless streaky bacon, diced
175 g (6 oz) tomatoes, skinned and chopped
175 g (6 oz) dried haricot beans, soaked overnight and drained
1.8 litres (3 pints) water
1 teaspoon dried basil
2 carrots, diced
2 celery sticks, chopped
250 g (8 oz) cabbage, shredded
salt and freshly ground black pepper
Meatballs:
500 g (1 lb) lean minced beef
2 tablespoons fresh white breadcrumbs
1 small onion, finely chopped
1 teaspoon powdered thyme
1 egg, beaten
salt and freshly ground black pepper
To serve:
1 tablespoon tomato purée
finely grated Parmesan cheese
French bread

Heat the oil in a deep flameproof casserole. Add the onions and bacon and fry for 2–3 minutes. Add the tomatoes and drained haricot beans and cover with the water. Stir in the basil and season to taste.

Cover with a lid or some foil and cook in a preheated oven, 160°C (325°F), Gas Mark 3, for 2 hours.

Meanwhile, make the meatballs. Mix together all the ingredients until well blended. Use floured hands to mould the mixture into about 50 tiny meatballs.

Add the carrots, celery, cabbage and meatballs to the casserole. Cook for 30 minutes until the vegetables and meatballs are cooked.

Stir in the tomato purée and 2 tablespoons of grated Parmesan. Check the seasoning and serve with extra Parmesan and French bread.

Serves 8

right: tacos

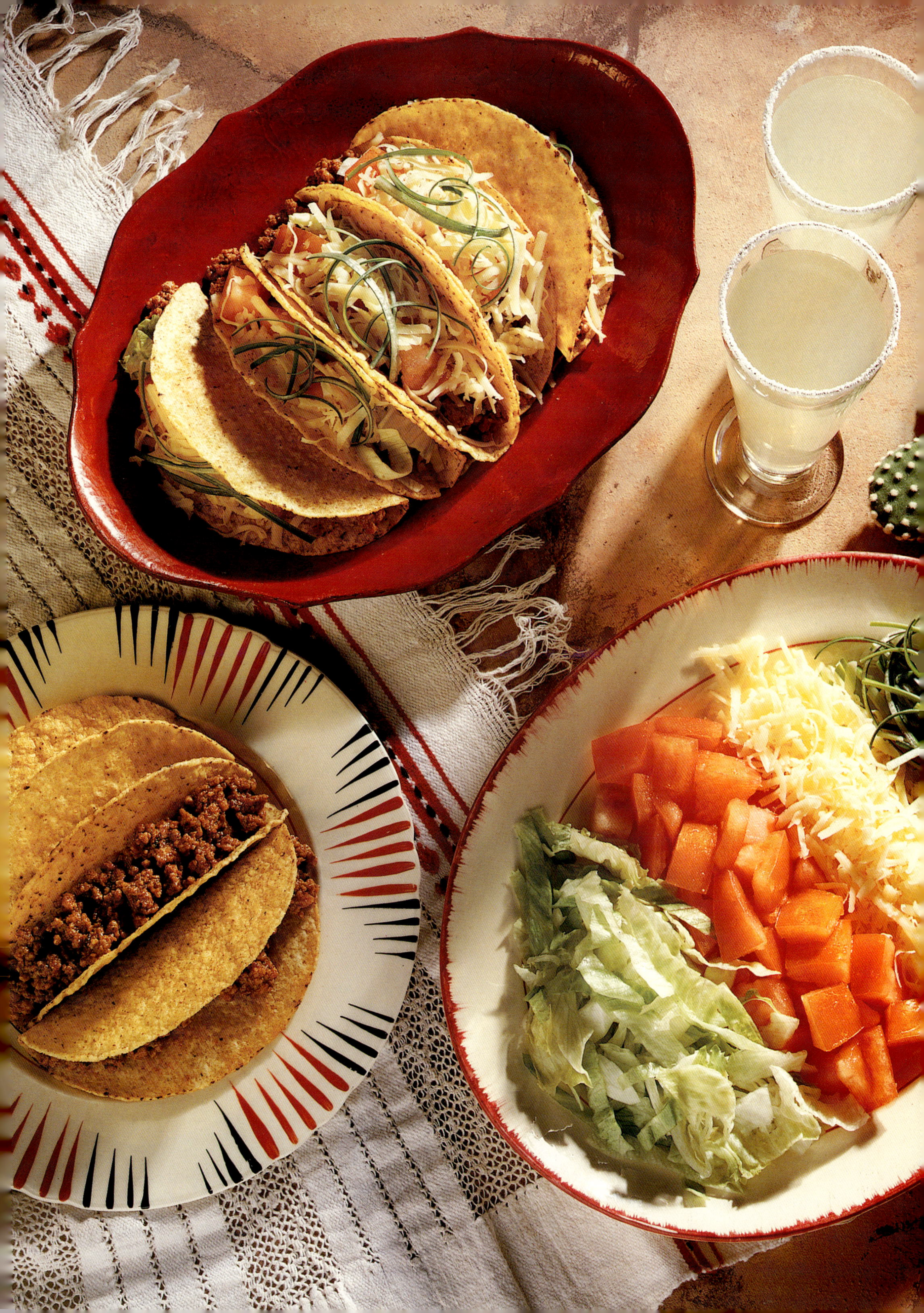

Aloo 'Chops'

1 large onion, finely chopped
1 cm (½ inch) piece of fresh root
   ginger, peeled and finely chopped
3 tablespoons oil
1 teaspoon ground coriander seeds
250 g (8 oz) lean minced beef
1 tablespoon raisins
1 tablespoon chopped coriander
1 kg (2 lb) mashed potatoes
flour, for coating
oil, for shallow-frying
salt

Fry the onion and ginger in the oil until golden. Add the ground coriander and minced beef and fry until brown. Add the raisins and salt to taste and simmer for 20 minutes until the meat is cooked. Drain off any fat in the pan. Stir in the fresh coriander and cool.

Divide the mashed potato into 8 portions. With well-floured hands, flatten a portion on one palm, put 3 teaspoons of the meat mixture into the centre and fold the potato over it. Form gently into a round patty.

Dip lightly in flour and shallow-fry, a few at a time, in hot oil until crisp and golden, turning carefully to brown the underside. Serve hot.

Serves 4

Cook's Tip: Use old potatoes for mashing. Don't overcook them and make sure you drain them properly after boiling or the end result will be sloppy.

Stuffed Mushrooms

4 large mushrooms
25 g (1 oz) butter
125 g (4 oz) minced pork
grated rind of 1 lemon
1 tablespoon fresh white breadcrumbs
2 tablespoons chopped sage
olive oil, for brushing
salt and pepper
watercress sprigs, to garnish

Wipe the mushrooms with a damp cloth, trim off the stalks and chop them finely. Heat the butter in a frying pan and sauté the mushroom stalks for a few minutes. Stir in the minced pork and sauté for about 5 minutes until evenly browned. Stir in the lemon rind, seasoning, breadcrumbs and sage.

Place the mushroom caps on a greased baking sheet and brush them with a little olive oil. Divide the pork filling between the mushrooms and then cook in a preheated oven, 160°C (325°F), Gas Mark 3, for 15–20 minutes.

Place each of the filled mushrooms on a small serving plate, garnish with watercress and serve hot.

Serves 2

Cocktail Meatballs with Barbecue Dip

500 g (1 lb) minced beef
1 onion, grated
50 g (2 oz) fresh white breadcrumbs
2 tablespoons chopped parsley
1 egg, lightly beaten
2 tablespoons oil
salt and pepper
Barbecue Dip:
25 g (1 oz) butter
1 onion, chopped
250 g (8 oz) can tomatoes
50 g (2 oz) pitted green olives
1 teaspoon dry mustard
few drops of Tabasco sauce
1 teaspoon Worcestershire sauce

Prepare the barbecue dip. Heat the butter in a frying pan and sauté the onion until softened. Add the remaining ingredients and simmer for 15 minutes. Allow the mixture to cool slightly, then blend in a liquidizer (or press through a sieve). Pour into a serving bowl and leave to cool.

To make the meatballs, mix together the minced beef, onion, breadcrumbs, seasoning and parsley and bind with the lightly beaten egg. With floured hands, shape the mixture into 2.5 cm (1 inch) balls. Heat the oil in a frying pan and cook the meatballs for about 5 minutes, turning them with a pair of tongs so that they are well-browned on all sides. Drain them on kitchen paper.

Insert a cocktail stick into each meatball and place on a tray with the bowl of barbecue dip.

Makes about 30

Layer Pie

4 tablespoons sunflower oil
500 g (1 lb) courgettes, sliced
250 g (8 oz) onions, thinly sliced
500 g (1 lb) lean minced steak
500 g (1 lb) tomatoes, skinned and sliced
½ teaspoon dried oregano
2 tablespoons chopped parsley
75 g (3 oz) Wensleydale cheese, very thinly sliced
salt and pepper
Topping:
300 ml (½ pint) natural yogurt
2 eggs, separated
pinch of grated nutmeg
50 g (2 oz) Wensleydale cheese, grated

Heat 3 tablespoons of the oil in a large frying pan and fry the courgettes for about 2 minutes on each side over a moderately high heat, until they begin to brown. Remove the courgettes, drain on kitchen paper and then set aside.

Heat the remaining oil and fry the onions over a moderate heat for 3 minutes. Add the minced steak and fry gently for 5 minutes, stirring frequently. Add the sliced tomatoes, oregano and parsley and season with salt and pepper. Bring to the boil, then cover the pan and simmer for 10 minutes, stirring occasionally.

In a shallow, greased baking dish, make layers of the meat sauce, fried courgettes and the cheese slices.

To make the topping, beat the yogurt, eggs, nutmeg and grated cheese together and pour over the courgette, meat and cheese layers. Bake in a preheated oven, 180°C (350°F), Gas Mark 4, for about 1 hour until the topping is a deep golden brown. Serve hot.

Serves 4

far left: aloo 'chops'

Minced Lamb and Parmesan Soufflé

Bake this soufflé in a large dish or in 6 individual ramekins if you prefer.

250 g (8 oz) lean minced lamb
1 small onion, finely chopped
2 courgettes, finely chopped
1 small green pepper, cored, deseeded and finely chopped
250 g (8 oz) can chopped tomatoes
1 garlic clove, crushed
25 g (1 oz) soya margarine
25 g (1 oz) wholemeal flour
200 ml (7 fl oz) skimmed milk
3 eggs, separated
40 g (1½ oz) finely grated Parmesan cheese
salt and pepper

In a non-stick pan over a medium heat, fry the minced lamb without added fat, stirring for 3–4 minutes until it is evenly coloured. Pour off any excess fat. Stir in the onion, courgettes, green pepper and canned tomatoes. Add the garlic and season with salt and pepper. Reduce the heat, cover the pan and simmer gently for 10–15 minutes. Spoon the meat mixture into a 1.2 litre (2 pint) soufflé dish or into 6 individual ramekins.

Put the margarine, flour and milk in a small saucepan and whisk over a moderate heat until the mixture has thickened. Beat in the egg yolks with about 25 g (1 oz) of the cheese and a little salt and pepper. Whisk the egg whites until they are stiff and gently fold them into the sauce.

Cover the meat mixture evenly with the sauce and sprinkle the remaining Parmesan cheese on top. Bake in a preheated oven, 190°C (375°F), Gas Mark 5, for 25 minutes for a large soufflé, or for about 10 minutes for small ones, until they are well risen and golden. Serve the soufflé(s) immediately.

Serves 4–6

Thai Stuffed Omelette

3 tablespoons vegetable oil
1 garlic clove, crushed
125 g (4 oz) lean minced pork
1 tablespoon nam pla (fish sauce)
½ tablespoon sugar
125 g (4 oz) finely chopped onion
1 tomato, skinned and chopped
3 eggs, beaten
coriander leaves, to garnish
freshly ground black pepper

In a saucepan, heat 2 tablespoons of the oil. Add the garlic and stir-fry until it is golden brown. Add the minced pork, black pepper to taste, nam pla, sugar, onion and tomato, and continue to stir-fry for 5–10 minutes until all the ingredients are cooked and well blended.

Heat the remaining oil in a wok, tilting it so that the oil coats the entire surface. Pour away the excess oil. Pour in the beaten eggs and swirl them around the inside of the wok to form a thin skin.

Place the minced meat filling in the middle of the omelette, and then fold down the 4 sides to make a neat parcel. Slide the omelette out on to a serving dish, folded side down, garnish with coriander leaves and serve immediately.

Serves 1

left: minced lamb and Parmesan soufflés
below: Thai stuffed omelette

Mince Kebab

750 g (1½ lb) minced beef
2 garlic cloves, crushed
2 green chillies, deseeded and finely chopped
1 teaspoon salt
oil
1 small lettuce, shredded, to serve

To garnish:
sprigs of coriander
lemon quarters

In a bowl, mix together the minced beef, garlic, chillies and salt. Knead, using your hands to blend evenly. Divide the mixture into 16 equal-sized portions.

Rub a chopstick, or a utensil of similar size and thickness, with a little oil. Shape a portion of the meat around the pointed end of the chopstick to a length of about 10 cm (4 inches). Slide the kebab on to a greased baking sheet, twirling the chopstick as the meat slides off. Repeat with the remaining mixture.

Bake the mince kebabs on the top shelf of a preheated oven, 190°C (375°F), Gas Mark 5, for about 15–20 minutes. Serve them on a bed of shredded lettuce, garnished with coriander sprigs and some lemon quarters. Natural yogurt makes a good accompaniment.

Serves 4–6

below: mince kebab

Greek Keftedes

These are served throughout Greece and its islands and also in many Greek restaurants here.

2 eggs
50 g (2 oz) fresh white breadcrumbs
1 onion, grated
2 teaspoons chopped mint
2 tablespoons chopped parsley
1 tablespoon wine vinegar or lemon juice
1 kg (2 lb) minced lamb
flour, for coating
oil, for shallow-frying
salt and pepper

Break the eggs into a large mixing bowl and beat lightly with a fork. Stir in the breadcrumbs, onion, mint, parsley, wine vinegar or lemon juice and seasoning. Leave to stand for 15 minutes.

Add the minced lamb to the mixture in the bowl and, using your hands, mix all the ingredients thoroughly. With floured hands, shape the mixture into balls, about the size of an egg. Roll lightly in flour and flatten into patty shapes.

Heat the oil in a frying pan and fry the keftedes for about 5 minutes on each side until lightly browned and cooked through. Drain on kitchen paper and serve with a tomato sauce, if wished, and a crisp lettuce and tomato salad.

Serves 6

Dolmas

This traditional dish from Turkey, served as a main course, is a minced lamb mixture wrapped in vine leaves. You can buy canned vine leaves in specialist food stores and many large supermarkets but young cabbage leaves make an equally good substitute.

2 tablespoons oil
1 onion, chopped
125 g (4 oz) long-grain rice
900 ml (1½ pints) stock (see note) or water
500 g (1 lb) minced lamb
2 tablespoons chopped parsley
2 teaspoons chopped mint
2 teaspoons chopped dill
12 young cabbage leaves
salt and pepper
150 ml (5 fl oz) natural yogurt, to serve

Heat the oil in a large frying pan and sauté the onion until soft and translucent. Stir in the rice and cook, stirring, until lightly coloured. Add sufficient stock to cover the rice and cook over a low heat, stirring, until the rice is tender and the liquid is completely absorbed. Allow to cool and then mix in the minced lamb, parsley, mint, dill and seasoning.

Cook the cabbage leaves in boiling salted water for 2 minutes. Drain well and cut out the coarse central stalk. Spread the leaves out on a board and place a spoonful of the lamb mixture in the centre of each one. Fold the edges over the filling to make small, neat parcels.

Arrange the parcels, with the folds underneath, in a single layer in a shallow pan. Pour in sufficient stock to just cover the dolmas. Now cover with foil, pressing it close to the surface to keep the dolmas under the stock. Cook them gently over a low heat for about 1 hour.

With a draining spoon, lift the dolmas out of the stock on to a serving dish. Serve the yogurt separately.

Serves 4–6

Note: For the best results, you really need a stock made from veal or lamb bones. Do not use a beef stock as this is too strong. A stock made from a commercially-prepared chicken or herb stock cube can be used, but use only one cube to 900 ml (1½ pints) water.

Beef Samosas

The filling in these spicy snacks is not chilli-hot so, if you like, you can add about ½ teaspoon chilli powder or a finely chopped and deseeded fresh chilli to the meat mixture.

125 g (4 oz) plain flour
pinch of salt
50 ml (2 fl oz) water
1 tablespoon oil
oil, for deep-frying
Filling:
1 onion, finely chopped
1 garlic clove, crushed
2 tablespoons oil
1 teaspoon mustard seeds
2 green cardamoms
1 tablespoon ground cumin
1 tablespoon ground coriander
250 g (8 oz) lean minced beef
4 tablespoons water
salt and freshly ground black pepper

To make the dough, sift the flour into a bowl and add the salt. Make a well in the centre, then pour in the water and add the oil. Gradually stir the flour into the liquid to make a firm dough, then knead well until the dough is smooth and elastic. Wrap it in clingfilm and set it aside while you prepare the filling.

Fry the onion and garlic in the oil until the onion is softened but not browned. Add all the spices and cook for 2–3 minutes, stirring continuously. Stir in the minced beef and cook, breaking it up with a wooden spoon, until lightly fried. Season with salt and pepper and add the water, then bring to the boil and simmer until the water has evaporated. Set aside to cool.

To fill and shape the samosas, cut the dough into 8 equal portions and roll each piece in turn into a long narrow strip, each measuring about 23 x 8.5 cm (8 x 3½ inches). Trim one short end so that it is straight, and then place a little filling about 2.5 cm (1 inch) away from the edge. Fold one corner across the filling to cover it and form a triangular shape. Fold the filling and its cover over again in the opposite direction.

Continue folding the triangular pastry over and over, down the length of the pastry strip, until the whole strip is used. When you have only a short piece of dough left, trim the end straight, brush it with a little water and fold it neatly over the pastry, pressing it down well to seal in the filling.

Heat the oil for deep-frying to 180°C (350°F), or until a cube of bread browns in 30 seconds, and then fry the samosas, a few at a time, until they are golden brown, turning them over during cooking. Drain on kitchen paper and serve hot, warm or cold.

Makes 8

Lamb Samosas

These deep-fried snacks are eaten throughout India. Originally the pastry parcel contained meat at one end and something sweet at the other, rather like our traditional Cornish pasty which was a convenient way of carrying a packed lunch. The most popular filling is a spicy mixture of lamb, potatoes and peas.

1 tablespoon oil
1 garlic clove, crushed
175 g (6 oz) lean minced lamb
1 potato, grated
50 g (2 oz) peas
¼ teaspoon turmeric
½ teaspoon garam masala (optional)
oil, for deep-frying
salt and freshly ground black pepper
Pastry:
250 g (8 oz) plain flour
½ teaspoon salt
125 g (4 oz) margarine
4½ tablespoons milk

Heat the oil in a frying pan and sauté the garlic and lamb until browned on all sides. Stir in the potato, peas, turmeric and garam masala and cook, stirring to prevent the mixture from sticking, for about 5 minutes. Season to taste and leave to cool while making the pastry.

To make the pastry, sift the flour and salt into a bowl and rub in the butter or margarine until the mixture resembles fine breadcrumbs. Mix in the milk to form a tacky dough. With floured hands, break off balls, the size of walnuts, and roll each one out on a well-floured board to make a thin circle. (The mixture makes about 25 balls.)

In the centre of each circle place a heaped teaspoon of the lamb filling. Dampen the edges of the circles and then fold each one over to make a triangular-shaped patty completely enclosing the filling.

Heat the oil for deep-frying and fry the samosas, a few at a time, until they are crisp and golden brown. Remove with a slotted spoon, drain on kitchen paper and serve either hot or cold, but they taste better hot.

Makes about 25

Sloppy Joes

This popular American snack consists of a spiced beef mixture which can either be spooned on to cut toasted baps or used as a filling.

25 g (1 oz) butter
1 onion, finely chopped
1 green pepper, cored, deseeded and finely chopped
125 g (4 oz) mushrooms, thinly sliced
750 g (1½ lb) lean minced beef
50 ml (2 fl oz) chilli sauce
1 teaspoon Worcestershire sauce
1 teaspoon chopped parsley
salt and pepper

To serve:
8 baps, toasted and lightly buttered
1 small lettuce (optional)
8 celery sticks (optional)
2 tomatoes, thinly sliced (optional)
cucumber slices (optional)

Melt the butter in a large saucepan and then add the onion and fry gently for 10 minutes until tender, stirring frequently. Add the green pepper and mushrooms and cook for 3 minutes. Add the minced beef and cook until lightly browned. Remove from the heat, drain off any excess fat and then return the pan to a low heat.

Add the chilli sauce together with the Worcestershire sauce, parsley and seasoning. Stir well and then simmer slowly for about 5 minutes.

Fill or top the toasted baps with the beef mixture and serve on warm plates. If liked, serve with lettuce leaves, celery sticks and some sliced tomato and cucumber.

Makes 8 sandwiches

below: sloppy Joes

Pasta and Rice

Lentil Mince with Pasta

375 g (12 oz) lean minced beef
1 onion, chopped
1 large carrot, finely chopped
1 celery stick, chopped
75 g (3 oz) button mushrooms, sliced
250 g (8 oz) tomatoes, skinned and chopped
450 ml (¾ pint) beef stock
150 ml (¼ pint) red wine
50 g (2 oz) split red lentils
2 tablespoons tomato purée
2 tablespoons chopped parsley
250 g (8 oz) tagliatelle or spaghetti
salt and pepper
grated Parmesan cheese, to serve

In a large, non-stick pan, fry the mince without added fat, stirring until it is lightly coloured. Add the onion, carrot, celery and button mushrooms and stir for 2 minutes. Stir in the tomatoes, stock, wine, lentils and tomato purée. Add the parsley and season to taste with salt and pepper. Cover the pan and then simmer gently for 40 minutes, stirring the mixture occasionally.

Cook the tagliatelle or spaghetti in plenty of boiling, salted water for 10–12 minutes or until it is just tender. Drain the pasta well and divide between 4 hot serving plates. Spoon the beef and lentil sauce over the top. Sprinkle with a little grated Parmesan and then serve with a green salad.

Serves 4

Spaghetti alla Bolognese

This classic pasta dish is easy to make and always popular. If wished, you can make the Ragu Bolognese Sauce in advance and freeze it until required.

375 g (12 oz) spaghetti
25 g (1 oz) butter
1 quantity hot Ragu Bolognese Sauce (see right)
salt and freshly ground black pepper
grated Parmesan cheese, to serve

Cook the spaghetti in plenty of boiling salted water until it is *al dente* (just tender but still a little firm to the bite). Drain thoroughly.

Melt the butter and pour into a serving dish. Add 4 tablespoons of the ragu sauce, the drained cooked spaghetti and 2 tablespoons of grated Parmesan. Toss lightly to coat the pasta and season with black pepper. Pile the remaining sauce on top of the spaghetti and serve with the grated Parmesan.

Serves 4

Ragu Bolognese Sauce

2 tablespoons olive oil
50 g (2 oz) smoked streaky bacon, derinded and diced
1 onion, finely chopped
1 small carrot, diced
1 celery stick, diced
375 g (12 oz) finely minced beef
125 g (4 oz) chicken livers, finely chopped
4 tablespoons dry vermouth or white wine
300 ml (½ pint) beef stock
1 tablespoon tomato purée
grated nutmeg
2 tablespoons single cream
salt and pepper

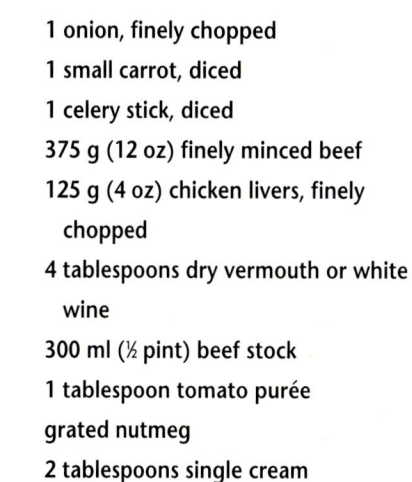

Heat the oil in a saucepan, add the bacon, onion, carrot and celery and sauté gently for 10 minutes, stirring frequently. Add the minced beef and cook, stirring, until browned. Stir in the chicken livers and the vermouth or wine. Bring to the boil and cook until the liquid has almost completely evaporated.

Stir in the stock and tomato purée, and season with salt, pepper and nutmeg to taste. Bring back to the boil, cover the pan and simmer for 1 hour, stirring occasionally. Adjust the seasoning to taste and stir in the cream.

Serve the ragu sauce with cooked spaghetti, tagliatelle, fettuccine or the pasta of your choice, sprinkled with grated Parmesan.

Serves 4–6

far left: lentil mince with pasta
left: spaghetti alla Bolognese

Lasagne al Forno

175 g (6 oz) green lasagne
1 quantity Ragu Bolognese Sauce
 (see page 25)
600 ml (1 pint) Béchamel Sauce
 (see right)
40 g (1½ oz) Parmesan cheese, grated
salt

Lightly butter a 20 cm (8 inch) square ovenproof dish, at least 3.5 cm (1½ inches) deep. Cook the lasagne in boiling salted water until *al dente* (just tender but still a little firm to the bite). Drain, rinse in cold water, then spread out on some clean tea-towels and pat dry with kitchen paper.

Spread a thin layer of ragu sauce across the base of the buttered dish, cover with a layer of lasagne, then a layer of ragu and finish with a thin layer of béchamel sauce and a sprinkling of Parmesan. Repeat these layers twice more, finishing with the cheese.

Bake in a preheated oven, 200°C (400°F), Gas Mark 6, for 20–25 minutes, until golden and bubbling. Serve immediately.

Serves 4–6

Béchamel Sauce

600 ml (1 pint) milk
1 small carrot, sliced
1 onion, quartered and stuck with
 4 cloves
6 peppercorns
1 bay leaf
50 g (2 oz) butter
50 g (2 oz) flour
salt and pepper

Put the milk in a saucepan with the carrot, onion, peppercorns and bay leaf. Heat the milk over a very low heat until just below boiling point, then reduce the heat and simmer for a few minutes.

Remove from the heat, cover the pan and set aside to stand and infuse for 15–30 minutes. Strain the milk, discarding the carrot, onion, spices and bay leaf.

Melt the butter in a clean saucepan, stir in the flour and beat well with a wooden spoon until a roux is formed. Gradually whisk or beat in the milk over a low heat until thickened and a smooth sauce is obtained. Season to taste with salt and pepper.

Makes 600 ml (1 pint)

Lamb Lasagne

Most of us are familiar with the classic baked lasagne made with a minced beef sauce and topped with a white sauce. However, you can make an equally delicious meal by substituting lamb for beef and topping it with a mixture of soured cream and grated cheese.

6 sheets of green lasagne
1 tablespoon oil
500 g (1 lb) minced lamb
1 large onion, chopped
2 carrots, chopped
425 g (14 oz) can tomatoes
150 ml (¼ pint) beef stock
1 tablespoon tomato purée
1 tablespoon chopped mint or
　1½ teaspoons dried mint
6 tablespoons soured cream
50 g (2 oz) mature Cheddar cheese, grated
1 tablespoon grated Parmesan cheese
salt and freshly ground black pepper
To garnish:
tomato slices
cucumber slices
sprigs of parsley

Cook the lasagne, a few sheets at a time, in plenty of boiling salted water with the oil, for about 10 minutes, or according to packet instructions, until *al dente*. Drain on kitchen paper.

Fry the lamb gently in a pan with no extra fat added until lightly browned. Add the onion and carrots and continue cooking for 2 minutes. Add the tomatoes, stock, tomato purée, mint and salt and pepper and bring to the boil. Simmer, uncovered, for 10 minutes until thickened. Adjust the seasoning to taste.

Place a layer of lasagne in a greased ovenproof dish. Cover with half of the lamb mixture. Repeat the layers of lasagne and lamb, ending with lasagne. Spread the soured cream over the lasagne and sprinkle with a mixture of grated Cheddar and Parmesan cheeses.

Cook in a preheated oven, 190°C (375°F), Gas Mark 5, for about 45 minutes or until golden brown and bubbling. Garnish with tomato and cucumber slices and parsley.

Serves 4

Variation: Use minced beef instead of lamb, replace the mint with oregano or marjoram and then add 125 g (4 oz) chopped button mushrooms with the canned tomatoes.

Minced Beef and Pasta Supper

This is a really quick and easy dish that you can rustle up when you come home from work. Serve it with some steamed green vegetables or, better still, a crisp salad of lettuce, tomatoes, peppers and red onion in a vinaigrette dressing.

25 g (1 oz) butter
1 onion, chopped
1 garlic clove, crushed
500 g (1 lb) lean minced beef
300 ml (½ pint) beef stock
250 g (8 oz) can baked beans
½ teaspoon dried mixed herbs
2 teaspoons paprika
2 teaspoons Worcestershire sauce
75 g (3 oz) pasta spirals or shells
salt and freshly ground black pepper
chopped parsley, to garnish

Heat the butter in a saucepan and gently sauté the onion and garlic until soft. Add the minced beef and cook over a high heat until lightly browned, stirring frequently. Add the remaining ingredients, except for the parsley, and season to taste.

Bring to the boil and cover the pan. Reduce the heat and simmer gently for 45 minutes until the meat is cooked and the pasta is tender. Serve immediately sprinkled with a little chopped parsley.

Serves 4–6

far left: lasagne al forno

Cannelloni

12 flat pieces pasta, about 7 x 10 cm (3 x 4 inches)
450 ml (¾ pint) Béchamel Sauce (see page 26)
300 ml (½ pint) passata
3 tablespoons grated Parmesan cheese
25 g (1 oz) butter
salt and pepper

Filling:
2 tablespoons oil
1 onion, chopped
1 garlic clove, crushed
250 g (8 oz) finely minced beef
250 g (8 oz) frozen chopped spinach, cooked and squeezed dry
40 g (1½ oz) grated Parmesan cheese
1 egg yolk

Butter a 20 cm (8 inch) square ovenproof dish. Cook the pasta in boiling salted water until *al dente* (just tender), stirring occasionally. Drain, spread on a clean tea-towel and pat dry with kitchen paper.

To prepare the filling, heat the oil in a saucepan, add the onion and garlic and fry gently until soft. Add the minced beef and cook, stirring, until well browned. Stir in the remaining ingredients. Bind the mixture with 2 tablespoons of the béchamel sauce and season well with salt and pepper.

Spread a rounded tablespoon of filling over each piece of pasta. Roll up loosely from the narrow side and place them, join side down, in the buttered dish. Pour over the passata and cover with the remaining béchamel sauce. Sprinkle with Parmesan and dot with butter.

Bake the cannelloni in a preheated oven, 200°C (400°F), Gas Mark 6, for 15–20 minutes until golden and bubbling.

Serves 4–6

Beef Noodle Casserole

You can use any green pasta noodles, such as fettuccine or tagliatelle, in this tasty supper dish.

175 g (6 oz) green noodles
750 g (1½ lb) lean minced beef
2 tablespoons oil
2 onions, chopped
1–2 garlic cloves, crushed
2 teaspoons cornflour
425 g (14 oz) can tomatoes
150 ml (¼ pint) beef stock
1 tablespoon soy sauce
1 tablespoon Worcestershire sauce
1 tablespoon tomato purée
1 teaspoon dried oregano
25 g (1 oz) butter
25 g (1 oz) flour
300 ml (½ pint) milk
40–50 g (1½–2 oz) mature Cheddar cheese, grated
salt and freshly ground black pepper

Cook the noodles in plenty of boiling salted water for about 8 minutes, or according to the packet instructions, until *al dente*. Drain well and set aside.

Cook the minced beef gently in the oil until lightly browned, stirring frequently. Add the onions and garlic and continue cooking for 3–4 minutes.

Blend the cornflour with a little of the juice from the canned tomatoes, then stir into the beef mixture with the tomatoes, soy sauce, Worcestershire sauce, tomato purée, oregano and salt and pepper. Bring to the boil, then reduce the heat and simmer for 10 minutes.

Put half of the noodles in the base of a casserole dish, cover with the meat mixture and then add the rest of the noodles.

Melt the butter in a pan, stir in the flour and cook for 1 minute, then gradually add the milk, still stirring, and bring to the boil for 1 minute. Add salt and pepper to taste and pour over the noodles.

Sprinkle with the cheese, cover the dish and cook in a preheated oven, 200°C (400°F), Gas Mark 6, for 15 minutes. Uncover and continue cooking for a further 10–15 minutes or until the top is golden brown and crisp.

Serves 4–5

Variation: You could add 125 g (4 oz) sliced mushrooms to the casserole. Plain noodles may be used instead of green ones, or you could try wholemeal ones.

far left: cannelloni
above: beef noodle casserole

Hot-tossed Noodles with Spicy Meat Sauce

This is an oriental version of spaghetti Bolognese and very tasty it is too!

2 tablespoons groundnut or vegetable oil
1 small onion, finely chopped
500 g (1 lb) lean minced beef
150 ml (¼ pint) beef stock
2 tablespoons soy sauce
2 tablespoons tomato purée
1 tablespoon sherry vinegar or wine vinegar
½ teaspoon chilli powder, or to taste
½ teaspoon sugar
¼ teaspoon garlic salt
250 g (8 oz) packet medium egg noodles
sprigs of marjoram, to garnish

Heat a wok until hot. Add the oil and heat over a moderate heat until hot. Add the onion and stir-fry over a gentle heat for 2–3 minutes until softened. Add the minced beef, increase the heat to high and then stir-fry for about 5 minutes, until lightly browned.

Now add all of the remaining ingredients, except the noodles and marjoram, and bring to the boil, stirring. Lower the heat, cover the wok with a lid and simmer for 10–15 minutes until the mixture thickens, stirring frequently.

Meanwhile, cook the egg noodles according to the packet instructions, until *al dente*. Drain well, then turn out into a warmed large serving bowl. Add the meat sauce to the noodles. Garnish with marjoram sprigs and serve at once.

Serves 4

above: hot-tossed noodles with spicy meat sauce
right: Ma Po's minced beef

Ma Po's Minced Beef

Tofu (beancurd) is a highly nutritious food, often used in Oriental cooking as a form of inexpensive protein. In this delicious recipe it helps to make a little meat go a long way.

2 teaspoons cornflour
150 ml (¼ pint) water
2 tablespoons soy sauce
2 tablespoons hoisin sauce
2 teaspoons chilli sauce
1 teaspoon soft dark brown sugar
3 tablespoons groundnut or vegetable oil
125 g (4 oz) lean minced beef
2 teaspoons black bean sauce
6 medium flat mushrooms, peeled and quartered
4 spring onions, sliced thinly into rounds
3 garlic cloves, crushed
297 g (10½ oz) packet tofu (beancurd), drained, dried and diced
1 tablespoon sesame oil
boiled rice or fried noodles, to serve

Blend the cornflour in a jug with 3 tablespoons of the water, then add the remaining water, the soy, hoisin and chilli sauces and the sugar. Stir well to combine.

Heat a wok until hot. Add the oil and heat over a moderate heat until hot. Add the minced beef and black bean sauce, the mushrooms and half of the spring onions. Increase the heat to high and then stir-fry for 3–4 minutes.

Add the garlic, cornflour mixture and tofu and bring to the boil, stirring constantly until thickened and glossy. Stir-fry for a further 2 minutes, then sprinkle over the remaining spring onions and the sesame oil. Serve immediately with boiled rice or fried noodles.

Serves 4

Veal with Chilli

If you don't want to use veal in this recipe, you could substitute lean minced beef or even minced pork. Canned red kidney beans make a good alternative to dried ones if you are in a hurry.

250 g (8 oz) dried red kidney beans, soaked overnight and drained
1 small onion, quartered
1 bouquet garni (thyme, parsley and bay leaf)
1 tablespoon sunflower oil
2 onions, sliced
1 garlic clove, finely chopped
500 g (1 lb) minced pie veal
1 tablespoon wholewheat flour
1 teaspoon dried oregano
1 teaspoon paprika
1 teaspoon chilli powder (or to taste)
2 red peppers, cored, deseeded and thinly sliced
375 g (12 oz) tomatoes, skinned and sliced
300 ml (½ pint) chicken stock
salt and freshly ground black pepper
boiled rice, to serve

Put the drained red kidney beans, quartered onion and bouquet garni into a pan. Cover with water, bring to the boil and boil rapidly for 15 minutes. Lower the heat and simmer for 1 hour until tender. Drain and remove the bouquet garni.

Heat the oil in a flameproof casserole and fry the sliced onions and garlic over a moderate heat for 2 minutes, stirring occasionally. Add the minced veal, stir well and cook for 5 minutes. Stir in the flour, salt and pepper, oregano, paprika and chilli powder and cook for 2 more minutes. Add the red peppers, tomatoes and kidney beans together with the stock.

Bring to the boil, then cover the casserole and simmer very gently for about 45 minutes, stirring occasionally. Adjust the seasoning to taste if necessary before serving with plain boiled rice.

Serves 4

Ants Climbing Trees

This dish gets its name from the minced pork ('ants') clinging to the noodles ('trees'). Transparent cellophane noodles are the traditional noodles used in this recipe, but ordinary egg noodles will be just as good.

250 g (8 oz) minced pork
200 g (7 oz) packet fine egg noodles
2 tablespoons groundnut or vegetable oil
4 spring onions, trimmed and chopped
250 ml (8 fl oz) hot chicken stock
2 spring onions, finely chopped, to garnish
Marinade:
2 tablespoons soy sauce
1 tablespoon dry sherry or sherry vinegar
1 tablespoon groundnut or vegetable oil
1 teaspoon sesame oil
1 teaspoon chilli sauce
½ teaspoon sugar
pinch of salt

Whisk the marinade ingredients together in a bowl. Add the minced pork and stir well to mix. Cover the bowl and leave to marinate in a cool place for about 30 minutes.

Meanwhile, cook the fine egg noodles, according to the packet instructions, and drain thoroughly.

Heat the wok until hot. Add the oil and heat over a moderate heat until hot. Add the marinated pork and spring onions and stir-fry for about 5 minutes or until the meat loses its pink colour.

Pour in the stock and bring to the boil, stirring constantly, and then add the drained noodles. Stir-fry for 1 minute or until all of the liquid is absorbed and the noodles are hot. Garnish with the chopped spring onions and serve hot.

Serves 3–4

right: Middle Eastern lamb

Middle Eastern Lamb

500 g (1 lb) minced lamb
¼ teaspoon mixed herbs
seasoned flour, for coating
1 large onion, sliced
2 tablespoons oil
1 leek, cleaned, trimmed and sliced
1 aubergine, diced
425 g (14 oz) can tomatoes
1 cinnamon stick
pinch of ground coriander
few cumin seeds
4 tablespoons water
150 ml (¼ pint) white wine
salt and freshly ground black pepper
boiled rice or noodles, to serve

Mix the lamb with the seasoning and mixed herbs in a bowl. Form into small balls and coat with seasoned flour.

Sauté the onion in the oil until tender, then add the leek and cook very gently over a low heat. Transfer the leek and onion to a casserole.

Fry the lamb balls in the pan until golden brown and then remove and transfer them to the casserole. Put the aubergine, tomatoes, cinnamon, coriander and cumin seeds in the pan with the water and wine. Bring to the boil and then pour over the lamb.

Cover the casserole and cook in a preheated oven, 180°C (350°F), Gas Mark 4, for 1 hour. Check the seasoning and adjust if necessary just before serving with plenty of plain boiled rice or noodles.

Serves 4

Risotto

A risotto is a traditional Italian rice dish. Here is a basic recipe using minced pork, which you can change as you see fit. If adding ingredients that cook very quickly, such as canned artichoke hearts, button mushrooms or ripe olives, toss them into the rice at the last minute. If the vegetables need longer cooking, such as carrots, celery or celeriac, sauté them with the onions, garlic and rice at the beginning.

4 tablespoons olive oil
1 large red pepper, cored, deseeded and diced
1 large green pepper, cored, deseeded and diced
1 large onion, chopped
2 garlic cloves, crushed
4 celery sticks, sliced
500 g (1 lb) minced pork
250 g (8 oz) long-grain rice
600 ml (1 pint) boiling chicken stock
125 g (4 oz) frozen French beans
4 tablespoons chopped fresh basil or marjoram
salt and freshly ground black pepper
freshly grated Parmesan cheese, to serve

Heat the oil in a large heavy-based frying pan and cook the peppers, onion and garlic until softened but not browned. Stir in the celery and minced pork and cook until the meat is lightly browned.

Add the rice and continue cooking until the grains begin to turn translucent. Add some of the stock to the pan together with the seasoning and bring to the boil. As soon as the liquid boils, reduce the heat to a gentle simmer.

Cover the pan and cook over a moderate heat for 10 minutes, adding more stock as and when necessary. Do not allow the rice mixture to become too dry or to stick to the pan. Add the beans to the pan and bring back to the boil, then cover the pan and simmer for a further 10–15 minutes until the rice is tender but not sticky and all the liquid has been absorbed.

Just before serving the risotto, stir in the herbs and fluff up the rice with a fork. Serve immediately with a bowl of grated Parmesan.

Serves 4

below: risotto
right: fried rice with pork and prawns

Fried Rice with Pork and Prawns

Oriental-style fried rice makes a good supper dish. Serve the rice straight from the pan or in one big serving bowl with small bowls and chopsticks for each person so that everyone dips into the pan of rice to take what they want.

4 Chinese dried mushrooms
4 tablespoons oil
few drops of sesame oil
1 garlic clove, crushed
250 g (8 oz) long-grain rice
500 g (1 lb) minced pork
250 g (8 oz) can water chestnuts, drained and sliced
4 tablespoons soy sauce
450 ml (¾ pint) water
250 g (8 oz) peeled cooked prawns
2 eggs, beaten
4 spring onions, chopped

Put the dried mushrooms in a small basin and pour in enough hot water to cover them. Put a saucer on top to keep them submerged in the water and leave them to soak for about 15 minutes.

Meanwhile, heat 3 tablespoons of the oil in a heavy-based saucepan or wok and add the sesame oil and garlic. Stir in the rice and stir-fry until the grains are translucent. Add the minced pork and continue to cook, stirring frequently, until the pork is lightly cooked.

While the pork is cooking, drain the mushrooms and then slice them thinly. Add them to the pan with the water chestnuts and pour in the soy sauce. Stir in the water and then bring to the boil. Reduce the heat and cover the pan tightly, then leave to simmer for 10 minutes. Add the prawns to the rice mixture but do not stir. Cover the pan and cook for a further 10 minutes.

Heat the remaining oil in a large frying pan until really hot and then pour in the beaten eggs and cook quickly until they are bubbling and beginning to set. Lift the sides of the omelette to allow any uncooked egg to run underneath on to the pan. When the omelette is set and the underneath is well browned, turn it over with a large fish slice. If you are not confident that you can do this, invert it on to a large plate and then slide it back into the pan. When cooked, slide the omelette out on to a plate which is lined with kitchen paper.

Cut the omelette first into thin strips, and then across into 2.5 cm (1 inch) lengths. When the rice is cooked, fork the prawns, omelette pieces and spring onions into the grains and serve immediately.

Serves 4

Mexican Beef with Lime Rice

500 g (1 lb) lean minced beef
2 tablespoons vegetable oil
1 onion, finely chopped
1 green or red pepper, cored, deseeded and diced
2 garlic cloves, finely chopped
1 tablespoon tomato purée
½ teaspoon chilli powder (or to taste)
1 teaspoon cumin seeds, toasted
150 g (5 oz) frozen sweetcorn kernels
250 g (8 oz) cooked or canned kidney beans
450 ml (¾ pint) beef stock
250 g (8 oz) long-grain rice
300 ml (½ pint) water
juice of 2 limes
3 tablespoons finely chopped coriander
salt and pepper

Fry the minced beef in the oil until lightly browned. Add the onion, green or red pepper and garlic and fry until just softened.

Add the tomato purée, chilli powder, cumin seeds, sweetcorn, beans and stock. Season to taste and bring to the boil, then simmer for 45 minutes, stirring occasionally.

Put the rice, water, lime juice and ½ teaspoon of salt in a saucepan. Bring to the boil and stir once. Cover and simmer for 15 minutes. Fluff up the rice with a fork and stir in the coriander. Serve with the beef.

Serves 4

Chilli con Carne

2 tablespoons vegetable oil
3 onions, chopped
1 red pepper, cored, deseeded and diced
2 garlic cloves, crushed
500 g (1 lb) lean minced beef
450 ml (¾ pint) beef stock
½–1 teaspoon chilli powder,
500 g (1 lb) cooked or canned kidney beans
425 g (14 oz) can chopped tomatoes
½ teaspoon ground cumin
250 g (8 oz) long-grain rice
salt and freshly ground black pepper

Heat the oil in a pan, add the onions, red pepper and garlic and gently fry until soft. Add the minced beef and cook until just coloured. Blend in the stock and add the chilli powder, kidney beans, tomatoes and cumin. Season to taste with salt and pepper.

Bring to the boil, then reduce the heat, cover the pan and simmer gently over a low heat for 50–60 minutes, stirring occasionally.

Meanwhile, boil the rice in plenty of salted water, according to the packet instructions, until just tender. Drain and serve with the chilli con carne.

Serves 4

far left: Mexican beef with lime rice
right: chilli con carne

Paprika Beef with Rice

2 tablespoons vegetable oil
50 g (2 oz) butter
1 onion, thinly sliced
1 garlic clove, crushed
2 celery sticks, thinly sliced
500 g (1 lb) lean minced beef
1 tablespoon flour
1 tablespoon paprika
1 bay leaf
300 ml (½ pint) beef stock
250 g (8 oz) long-grain rice
125 g (4 oz) button mushrooms, sliced
3 tablespoons soured cream
salt and freshly ground black pepper
1 tablespoon finely chopped parsley, to garnish

Heat the oil and half of the butter in a pan and gently fry the onion, garlic and celery for 4 minutes, stirring occasionally. Add the minced beef and fry for 4 minutes, stirring occasionally, until evenly browned. Stir in the flour and paprika, and cook over a medium heat for 2 more minutes.

Add the bay leaf and beef stock, season to taste and bring to the boil. Cover the pan and simmer gently for about 50 minutes.

Meanwhile, boil the rice in plenty of salted water until it is just tender, then drain thoroughly.

Fry the button mushrooms in the remaining butter for 5 minutes.

Remove the bay leaf from the beef mixture, stir in the soured cream and heat through very gently without boiling. Transfer the beef mixture to a large serving dish and surround with a border of rice. Top with the mushrooms and serve garnished with chopped parsley.

Serves 4

Alabama Chilli

1 tablespoon oil
500 g (1 lb) lean minced beef
2 onions, diced
1 carrot, diced
1 red or green pepper, cored, deseeded and diced
1 fresh chilli, deseeded and diced
425 g (14 oz) can tomatoes
2–3 tablespoons tomato purée
150 ml (¼ pint) stock
1 bay leaf
½ teaspoon chilli powder
½ teaspoon dried mixed herbs
250 g (8 oz) packet frozen sweetcorn
425 g (14 oz) can kidney beans, drained
salt and freshly ground black pepper
boiled rice or pasta, to serve

Heat the oil in a frying pan and add the minced beef. Cook gently over a medium heat until browned and then transfer to a casserole.

Sauté the onion, carrot, pepper and chilli until softened and add to the beef in the casserole. Add the remaining ingredients, except for the sweetcorn and kidney beans, and simmer for a further 15 minutes. Add the sweetcorn and kidney beans and then simmer for 5 minutes until heated through.

Remove the bay leaf and adjust the seasoning to taste. Serve the chilli with plain boiled rice or pasta.

Serves 4

far left: paprika beef with rice
above: *Alabama chilli*

Pastry, Pizzas and Pancakes

Meat Puffs

In this unusual recipe, the spicy minced beef mixture is actually mixed into the batter before frying. Serve these little meat puffs as a hot party canapé.

- 3 tablespoons self-raising flour
- 3 eggs, beaten
- 5–6 tablespoons water
- 250 g (8 oz) lean minced beef
- 1 bunch spring onions, trimmed and finely sliced
- 1 green chilli, deseeded and finely chopped
- 1 teaspoon turmeric
- vegetable oil, for frying
- salt, to taste

Sift the flour into a bowl, add the eggs and then beat well to combine. Gradually add enough water to make a thick, creamy batter, beating well all the time.

Stir in the minced beef, spring onions, chilli, turmeric and salt to taste; the mixture should have the consistency of stiff porridge. Leave to stand in a warm place for 1 hour.

Heat about 1 cm (½ inch) depth of oil in a frying pan. When the oil is really hot, drop in spoonfuls of the meat mixture and fry on each side for 2 minutes until crisp and golden brown. Drain the puffs well and keep warm while cooking the remainder, adding more oil as required. Serve them immediately.

Serves 4

Beef and Olive Pasties

Perfect for packed lunches or picnics, these delicious savoury pasties are high in fibre and low in fat.

75 g (3 oz) plain flour
75 g (3 oz) wholemeal flour
1 teaspoon 'easy blend' dried yeast
25 g (1 oz) soy margarine
5 tablespoons skimmed milk
250 g (8 oz) lean minced beef
1 small onion, sliced thinly
2 firm tomatoes, skinned and chopped
1 garlic clove, crushed
8 stuffed green olives, halved
milk, to glaze
1 tablespoon bran
salt and freshly ground black pepper

To garnish:
sliced tomatoes
finely chopped basil

Combine the flours and yeast in a large bowl with a pinch of salt. Rub in the margarine evenly with the fingertips. Warm the milk until it is tepid, and then stir in just enough to make a firm dough.

Knead the dough until smooth. Place in a bowl, cover with a damp cloth and leave in a warm place until the dough is well risen and springy to the touch.

Meanwhile, fry the minced beef without added fat for about 5 minutes. Drain off any excess fat. Add the onion, tomatoes, garlic and olives and season with pepper.

Divide the dough into 4 portions and roll each one out on a lightly floured surface to make four 15 cm (6 inch) rounds. Place a tablespoon of the filling in the centre of each round. Brush the edges lightly with some milk. Fold over one side of the round to enclose the filling, making a semi-circle. Bring the bottom edge slightly over the top and then pinch them firmly together to seal.

Lift the pasties carefully on to a greased baking sheet and bend them slightly to form crescent shapes. Pierce a small hole in the centre of each pasty to allow steam to escape. Cover them with a cloth and leave them in a warm place for about 30 minutes to rise, until the dough is springy to the touch.

Brush the pasties lightly with some milk and then sprinkle the tops with bran. Bake in a preheated oven, 200°C (400°F), Gas Mark 6, for about 25 minutes until firm and golden brown. Garnish with sliced tomatoes and finely chopped basil.

Serves 2–4

left: meat puffs
above: beef and olive pasties

Savoury Plait

1 tablespoon vegetable oil
1 small onion, finely chopped
250 g (8 oz) lean minced beef
250 g (8 oz) minced pork and beef sausagemeat
3 teaspoons dried mixed herbs
1 egg
2 teaspoons soy sauce
400 g (13 oz) packet frozen puff pastry, defrosted
beaten egg, to glaze
salt and pepper
To garnish:
watercress sprigs
tomato quarters

Heat the oil in a small frying pan, add the onion and fry gently for about 5 minutes until softened and translucent.

Mix the minced beef, sausagemeat, herbs and seasoning in a large bowl and stir well. Mix in the fried onion. Beat the egg with the soy sauce and add to the mixture to bind.

On a floured surface, roll out the puff pastry to a rectangle, 25 x 40 cm (10 x 16 inches). Place on a baking sheet. Mark into 3 sections lengthways and spoon the meat mixture down the centre, to within 2.5 cm (1 inch) of the short edges. Cut the pastry down each side of the meat into diagonal strips, 1 cm (½ inch) apart, and brush lightly with beaten egg.

Take one strip from each side of the pastry and then cross them alternately over the meat. Continue folding over the pastry strips to give a plaited effect. Dampen the top and bottom ends of the plait with a little water and fold over to seal.

Brush all over with beaten egg and then bake in a preheated oven, 200°C (400°F), Gas Mark 6, for about 40–45 minutes until the pastry is crisp and golden. Serve hot or cold garnished with watercress sprigs and tomato quarters.

Serves 4–6

Minced Lamb Rolls

250 g (8 oz) lean minced lamb
1 small onion, finely chopped
2 tomatoes, skinned and chopped
2 teaspoons ground coriander
3 tablespoons finely chopped unsalted peanuts
8 sheets filo pastry
soya or sunflower oil, for brushing
poppy seeds, for sprinkling
salt and pepper

Tourtière

500 g (1 lb) lean minced pork
500 g (1 lb) minced pie veal
125 g (4 oz) salt pork or fat streaky bacon, diced
75 g (3 oz) butter
1 large onion, chopped
1 garlic clove, crushed
¼ teaspoon dried summer savory
50 ml (2 fl oz) water
375 g (12 oz) shortcrust pastry
salt and freshly ground black pepper

Mix the meats thoroughly. Heat the butter in a heavy frying pan and gently cook the onion and garlic until soft but not brown.

Stir in the mixed meats and dried summer savory and cook for about 5 minutes, stirring frequently. Season to taste with salt and pepper and stir in the water.

Roll out the pastry into 2 rounds to fit a deep 23 cm (9 inch) pie tin. Line the tin with one round of pastry and fill with the minced meat mixture. Cover with the other pastry round and seal the top crust to the bottom with cold water, then crimp the edges. Decorate with pastry leaves and cut steam vents.

Bake in a preheated oven, 190°C (375°F), Gas Mark 5, for 45 minutes until cooked and golden brown.

Serves 6–8

Place the minced lamb in a pan and dry-fry, stirring all the time, until lightly coloured. Drain off any fat. Stir in the onion and cook for 2 minutes, then add the tomatoes, coriander and seasoning. Simmer for 5 minutes until any liquid has evaporated. Stir in the nuts.

Lay 1 sheet of the filo pastry on a work surface. Brush lightly with oil and lay a second sheet on top. Place about one-quarter of the meat mixture down one short side of the pastry and roll up like a Swiss roll.

Place on a greased baking sheet. Repeat with the remaining pastry and filling to make 4 rolls in total. Brush lightly with oil and sprinkle with poppy seeds.

Bake the rolls in a preheated oven, 200°C (400°F), Gas Mark 6, for 15–20 minutes until they are golden brown and crisp. Serve hot.

Serves 4

far left: minced lamb rolls
above: tourtière

Empanada

A Spanish empanada can be a single pie or several individual pasties, with a crust which may be yeast based and a filling which varies according to the region. This recipe offers a colourful filling in an unsophisticated wrapping. You can, if wished, substitute a packet of bread mix quite successfully for the yeast dough.

Dough:
150 ml (¼ pint) lukewarm water
1 teaspoon sugar
3 teaspoons dried yeast
250 g (8 oz) strong plain flour
50 g (2 oz) butter, diced
½ teaspoon salt

Filling:
2 tablespoons olive oil
1 large green pepper, cored, deseeded and diced
1 green chilli, deseeded and chopped
2 garlic cloves, crushed
1 Spanish onion, chopped
175 g (6 oz) chorizo (spicy Spanish sausage), thinly sliced
500 g (1 lb) lean minced beef
50 g (2 oz) raisins
425 g (14 oz) can chopped tomatoes
4 hard-boiled eggs
salt and freshly ground black pepper

Make the dough. Pour the water into a basin and stir in the sugar, then sprinkle in the dried yeast and set aside in a warm place for about 30 minutes until the liquid is frothy.

Sift the flour into a bowl and add the butter. Mix in the salt and then rub the butter into the flour with the fingertips until the mixture resembles fine breadcrumbs. Give the yeast liquid a good stir, then add it to the flour and mix in to make a smooth dough.

Turn out the dough on to a lightly floured surface and knead thoroughly for about 10 minutes or until smooth and elastic. Place in a lightly oiled bowl, cover with clingfilm or a damp tea-towel and leave in a warm place until the dough has doubled in size.

Meanwhile, prepare the filling. Heat the oil and cook the green pepper, chilli, garlic and onion until the onion is soft but not browned, stirring well. Add the sliced chorizo, increase the heat slightly and fry, stirring frequently, for a few minutes. Add the minced beef and cook, breaking up the meat, until it is lightly browned. Season to taste with salt and pepper and stir in the raisins and tomatoes. Bring to the boil, then remove the pan from the heat. Roughly chop the eggs and add them to the meat mixture.

Briefly knead the risen dough, then cut about two-thirds off and roll it out to line a 25 cm (10 inch) ovenproof dish or shallow tin. Press the dough into the corners and make sure that there is plenty of extra dough around the edge.

Pile the prepared filling on top. Roll out the remaining dough to just cover the filling, place it on top and then brush with a little water. Fold over the edges of the dough lining the dish to seal in the filling completely.

Bake the pie in a preheated oven, 200°C (400°F), Gas Mark 6, for about 30–35 minutes until golden. Cut the pie into wedges to serve. Serve with a crisp green salad, if liked.

Serves 6–8

above left: empanada

Raised Pork Pie

This is not the easiest of pastry recipes to tackle, but the result justifies the effort involved. Once you have made hot-water crust pastry a few times you will find the task less daunting. A pork pie is excellent for including in a picnic meal or as part of a summer buffet.

1 kg (2 lb) minced pork
1 onion, finely chopped
2 tablespoons chopped fresh sage
1 tablespoon juniper berries, finely crushed
4 tablespoons brandy or dry sherry
beaten egg, to glaze
salt and freshly ground black pepper
Hot-water crust pastry:
500 g (1 lb) plain flour
½ teaspoon salt
175 g (6 oz) lard or block margarine
5 tablespoons milk
5 tablespoons water

Lightly grease an 18 cm (7 inch) loose-bottomed cake tin or special pork pie tin.

To prepare the filling, mix the pork with all the other ingredients (except the beaten egg), making sure the meat is well broken up and that all the ingredients are evenly combined. Set aside while you prepare the hot-water crust pastry.

Sift the flour and salt into a bowl and make a well in the centre. Put the fat in a saucepan with the milk and water. Heat gently until the fat melts, then increase the heat to the hottest setting and bring quickly to the boil. Immediately the liquid boils, pour it quickly into the dry ingredients. Tip in the flour and then use your hands to knead the dough together until smooth – take care as it will be very hot. Cut two-thirds of the dough off to line the tin, and cover the smaller portion with clingfilm. Leave it in the bowl over a saucepan of hot water.

Working quickly, knead the dough to make a smooth ball, then roll it out into a circle large enough to line the tin. Lift the pastry into the tin, holding the edge of the circle round the top of the tin. Carefully mould the pastry into the tin, making sure that you keep a good edge at the top. Press the pork mixture into the tin.

Roll out the reserved pastry to make a lid, then lift it over the pie and mould the edges together well to seal in the filling. Trim off any excess with a pair of kitchen scissors and use the trimmings to make pastry leaves to decorate the top of the pie. Flute the edge of the pastry between your fingers. Cut a small hole in the middle to allow the steam to escape, then glaze the top with a little beaten egg.

Bake the pie in a preheated oven, 180°C (350°F), Gas Mark 4, for 1½ hours. Leave the cooked pie to cool in the tin and then carefully push it out from the base. Serve cold.

Serves 8

Spiced Lamb Tart with Apricots

10 sheets filo pastry
5 tablespoons olive oil
1 onion, finely chopped
250 g (8 oz) lean minced lamb
1 teaspoon ground cumin
1 teaspoon ground coriander
2 teaspoons peeled and chopped fresh root ginger
125 g (4 oz) no-soak dried apricots, chopped
1 egg, beaten
75 ml (3 fl oz) Greek-style yogurt
salt and freshly ground black pepper

Brush each sheet of filo pastry with olive oil and arrange in layers, overlapping at different angles, in a 20 cm (8 inch) flan tin. Scrunch up the pastry around the edges.

Heat 1 tablespoon of the oil and fry the onion until soft. Add the lamb and cook until coloured. Stir in the spices and apricots. Cover and simmer gently for 10 minutes.

Beat together the egg and yogurt, season to taste and then stir into the meat mixture. Spoon the mixture into the pastry case.

Bake the tart in a preheated oven, 190°C (375°F), Gas Mark 5, for 20–25 minutes until the pastry is golden and the filling set. Serve hot.

Serves 4

Veal and Apple Pasties with Walnuts

Serve these unusual pasties either hot or cold. They go well with baked jacket potatoes and salad or a moist vegetable dish such as ratatouille.

400 g (13 oz) packet shortcrust pastry
beaten egg, to glaze
Filling:
500 g (1 lb) minced veal
1 large cooking apple, peeled, cored and diced
50 g (2 oz) chopped walnuts
1 small onion, finely chopped

2 tablespoons chopped mixed fresh
herbs, e.g. thyme, parsley, sage,
marjoram, rosemary
50 g (2 oz) raisins
salt and freshly ground black pepper

In a large bowl, mix all the filling ingredients together, making sure that the meat is well seasoned with salt and pepper.

Divide the pastry into 6 equal portions. Roll out each portion in turn into a 20 cm (8 inch) circle and put one-sixth of the filling in the centre of each one and dampen the edge. Fold the opposite sides of the pastry up to meet over the filling and pinch the edges together, making sure they are well sealed. Trim off any excess pastry and flute the seams. Place the pasties on a greased baking tray and brush them lightly with a little beaten egg.

Bake the pasties in a preheated oven, 200°C (400°F), Gas Mark 6, for 50–60 minutes until golden brown. Serve hot, or leave on a wire rack to cool.

Makes 6

left: spiced lamb tart with apricots
above right: beef and potato clock flan

Beef and Potato Clock Flan

125 g (4 oz) plain flour
75 g (3 oz) butter or margarine
125 g (4 oz) mashed potato
1 tablespoon sunflower oil
1 onion, chopped
250 g (8 oz) lean minced beef
1 teaspoon dried mixed herbs
1 tablespoon Worcestershire sauce
250 g (8 oz) can chopped tomatoes
1 tablespoon tomato purée
salt and freshly ground black pepper

Sift the flour and rub in the fat with your fingertips until the mixture resembles fine breadcrumbs. Stir in the mashed potato, season with salt and pepper and knead to a dough. Cover and chill in the refrigerator for 15 minutes.

Roll out the pastry on a floured surface and then use it to line a greased 23 cm (9 inch) flan dish, reserving the trimmings.

Heat the oil and fry the onion for 3–4 minutes. Add the minced beef and cook until lightly coloured. Add the herbs, Worcestershire sauce, tomatoes and tomato purée, and bring to the boil. Simmer for 3–4 minutes, and then spoon the beef mixture into the flan case.

Roll out the pastry trimmings and, using cutters or a sharp knife, cut out the numbers and hands of a clock. Arrange over the flan to resemble a clock face.

Bake the flan in a preheated oven, 180°C (350°F), Gas Mark 4, for 40–45 minutes. Serve hot.

Serves 4–6

Mexicali Pancakes

Golden corn pancakes, filled with spicy beef and pork and topped with soured cream and avocado, make a tempting meal for any occasion.

75 g (3 oz) cornmeal
25 g (1 oz) plain flour
2 eggs
300–450 ml (½–¾ pint) milk
oil or butter, for cooking
salt and freshly ground black pepper
Filling:
1 green pepper, cored, deseeded and diced
1 large onion, finely chopped
1 garlic clove, crushed
2 tablespoons peanut oil
250 g (8 oz) lean minced beef
250 g (8 oz) lean minced pork
150 ml (¼ pint) boiling beef stock
400 g (13 oz) can chopped tomatoes
1 teaspoon chilli powder (optional)
Topping:
2 large ripe avocado pears, peeled, stoned and diced
juice of ½ lemon
1 garlic clove, crushed
150 ml (¼ pint) soured cream
2 tablespoons chopped coriander leaves

To make the pancake batter, put the cornmeal in a bowl with the flour and plenty of salt and pepper. Make a well in the middle, break the eggs into it and beat well, gradually working in the dry ingredients and, at the same time, pouring in 300 ml (½ pint) of the milk, a little at a time. Beat until the batter is quite smooth, and then set aside to stand for at least 30 minutes while you prepare the filling.

Gently fry the pepper, onion and garlic in the oil until softened. Add the minced meats and cook over a moderate heat, breaking up the meat with a spoon as it cooks, until lightly browned. Pour in the stock, then stir in the tomatoes and bring to the boil. Add the chilli powder (if used) and reduce the heat to a bare simmer. Leave to cook while you make the pancakes.

Heat a little oil or butter in a frying pan. Give the batter a good stir, adding a little extra milk to thin it down, and pour enough into the pan to coat the base generously – the pancakes should not be too thin. Cook until the mixture is set and golden underneath, then turn the pancake over and cook the other side. Keep warm while you cook the other pancakes in the same way – you should have 8 pancakes. Layer the pancakes with kitchen paper to prevent them sticking together.

Sprinkle the diced avocadoes with some lemon juice to prevent them discolouring and stir in the garlic and soured cream.

Fill the pancakes with the meat mixture, fold them in half and arrange them in a large warmed serving dish. Spoon the avocado mixture down the middle and sprinkle with chopped coriander. Serve at once.

Serves 4

Chilli Calzone

A calzone is an Italian creation, a sort of pizza which is folded in half to enclose a filling in a light and crisp bread crust. Here the bread crust is folded around a chilli-spiced beef mixture which is topped with Italian cheese.

½ x 560 g (20 oz) packet bread mix

Filling:
2 tablespoons olive oil
2 garlic cloves, crushed
1 large onion, chopped
500 g (1 lb) lean minced beef
2 tablespoons ground coriander
1 tablespoon chilli powder
325 g (11 oz) can sweetcorn, drained
375 g (12 oz) mozzarella cheese, sliced
1 teaspoon dried marjoram
½ teaspoon chopped dried thyme
salt and freshly ground black pepper

Make up the bread mix, according to the packet instructions but using half the quantity of water. Roll out the dough to make a large circle, about 35 cm (14 inches) in diameter. Grease a baking tray or roasting tin and lay the dough on top – it will eventually be folded in half like a pasty, so don't worry if it seems far too large for the container at this stage.

For the filling, heat the oil in a large frying pan and fry the garlic and onion until soft but not browned. Stir in the beef and cook briefly, then mix in the coriander and chilli powder. Stir well and season to taste with salt and pepper.

Add the sweetcorn, then remove the pan from the heat and spread the mixture over half the rolled-out dough. Top with the mozzarella and sprinkle with herbs. Brush the edges of the dough with a little water and fold the uncovered side over to enclose the filling completely in a half-moon shape. Pinch the edges together to seal in the filling and cut off any excess.

Bake the calzone in a preheated oven, 220°C (425°F), Gas Mark 7, for about 40 minutes or until browned and cooked through. Serve hot, cut into wedges.

Serves 4–6

Peppered Beef Pizza

½ x 275 g (9 oz) packet bread mix
Topping:
500 g (1 lb) lean minced beef
1 garlic clove, crushed
1 small onion, grated
2 tablespoons tomato purée
1 teaspoon paprika
125 g (4 oz) button mushrooms, sliced
1 red pepper, cored, deseeded and sliced into rings
1 green pepper, cored, deseeded and sliced into rings
250 g (8 oz) mozzarella cheese, thinly sliced
50 g (2 oz) can anchovy fillets, cut in half lengthways
a few black olives
salt and freshly ground black pepper

Make up the bread mix, according to the packet instructions but using half the quantity of water. Roll it out into a 25 cm (10 inch) circle and place this on a greased baking tray. Fold the edge back to form a neat rim, then leave the dough, covered with a piece of clingfilm, in a warm place while you prepare the topping.

Mix the minced beef with the garlic, onion and tomato purée, and then stir in the paprika and salt and ground black pepper to taste.

Uncover the pizza base and then spread the mince mixture on top, spreading it evenly and patting it into shape like a big hamburger. Arrange the mushrooms on top with the pepper rings. Cover with the mozzarella cheese and arrange the anchovies and olives in a lattice pattern on top. Sprinkle the anchovy oil over the pizza.

Bake the pizza in a preheated oven, 220°C (425°F), Gas Mark 7, for 40–45 minutes until the topping is golden and the base is cooked through. Serve piping hot, cut into large wedges.

Serves 4–6

far left: mexicali pancakes

Burgers, Meatballs and Meat Loaves

Mince and Mushroom Burgers

500 g (1 lb) lean minced beef
1 small onion, finely chopped
175 g (6 oz) open cup mushrooms, finely chopped
125 g (4 oz) fresh wholemeal breadcrumbs
finely grated rind of ½ lemon
1 egg, beaten
2 tablespoons wholemeal flour
salt and pepper

To serve:
12 wholemeal pitta breads
1 lettuce, shredded
4 firm tomatoes, sliced

In a bowl, mix together the minced beef, onion, mushrooms and breadcrumbs. Stir in the lemon rind and enough beaten egg to bind the mixture. Season lightly with salt and pepper. Dust your hands with the flour and form the mixture into 12 flat burgers.

Cook the burgers over hot coals on a barbecue, or under a

preheated hot grill, turning them once, until they are lightly browned and are thoroughly cooked. To serve, split open the warm pitta breads and place the burgers inside with some shredded lettuce and tomato slices.

Serves 6

Chillied Meat Koftas with Mint

The amount of hot chilli can be adjusted according to taste in this recipe. If you cannot obtain fresh chillies, you can use dried ones instead.

500 g (1 lb) lean minced lamb
1 onion, grated or minced
2 garlic cloves, crushed
2 small red chillies, deseeded and chopped
3 tablespoons chopped mint
finely grated rind and juice of
   1 small lime
wholemeal flour, for shaping
soya or sunflower oil, for brushing
salt and pepper
To garnish:
lime wedges
mint leaves
natural yogurt

Mix together the minced lamb, onion, garlic, chillies, mint, lime rind and juice. Season with salt and pepper. Using lightly floured hands, shape the mixture into 8 small sausage shapes and then thread them on to 4 skewers.

Place the koftas over hot coals on a barbecue, or under a preheated moderately hot grill, and cook for about 10 minutes, turning them occasionally, until they are evenly cooked. Brush them with oil while cooking, if necessary, to prevent them drying out. Serve the koftas hot, garnished with lime wedges and mint leaves, with some natural yogurt to spoon over them.

Serves 4

far left: mince and mushroom burgers
above: chillied meat koftas with mint

Porky Oatmeal Sausages

These delicious high-fibre, home-made sausages will soon be snapped up from the barbecue by your guests.

375 g (12 oz) lean minced pork
1 onion, finely chopped or minced
40 g (1½ oz) rolled oats
50 g (2 oz) wholemeal breadcrumbs
75 g (3 oz) mature Cheddar cheese, grated
1 egg, beaten
1 tablespoon chopped sage
1 teaspoon German mustard
wholemeal flour, for rolling
vegetable oil, for brushing
salt and pepper

Put the minced pork in a large bowl and break it up with a fork. Stir in the onion, oats, breadcrumbs and cheese, and mix thoroughly until the ingredients are evenly blended. Stir in the beaten egg, sage and mustard and season with salt and pepper. Using lightly floured hands, form the mixture into 12 small sausage shapes. Chill them in the refrigerator, covered, until needed.

Place the sausages on a hot barbecue or under a preheated hot grill and cook for about 6–8 minutes, turning them frequently, until they are golden brown and thoroughly cooked. Brush lightly with vegetable oil if necessary. Serve hot.

Makes 12

Swedish Meat Cakes

3 slices white bread, crusts removed
150 ml (¼ pint) soda water
250 g (8 oz) minced veal
250 g (8 oz) minced pork
50 g (2 oz) cooked ham, finely chopped
1 teaspoon juniper berries, crushed
2 egg yolks
vegetable oil, for brushing
salt and freshly ground black pepper
To serve:
4 large slices rye bread, spread with unsalted butter
1 onion, cut into thin rings
2 pickled cucumbers, cut into fingers
½ fresh cucumber, sliced
2 tablespoons capers
150 ml (¼ pint) soured cream

Break the bread into rough pieces and put into a shallow dish with the soda water. Set aside to soak for about 20 minutes.

Mix the minced and chopped meats with the juniper berries, egg yolks and salt and pepper to taste. Add the moistened bread. Beat, or work the mixture with your hands, until smooth. Form into 4 burger shapes or meat cakes. Chill in the refrigerator for 30 minutes.

Brush the meat cakes with some oil, place on a preheated barbecue grill over hot coals and cook for 4 minutes. Turn the meat cakes over, brush lightly with oil and cook for a further 4 minutes. Alternatively, cook under a preheated hot grill.

Place a slice of rye bread on each serving plate. Top each slice with a hot meat cake and garnish with a few onion rings, some pickled and fresh cucumber and a some of capers. Add a swirl of soured cream to each plate and serve.

Serves 4

Japanese Pork Balls with Dipping Sauce

500 g (1 lb) lean minced pork
125 g (4 oz) open cup mushrooms, chopped
3 spring onions, finely chopped
1 egg, beaten
50 g (2 oz) fresh wholemeal breadcrumbs
2 teaspoons soy sauce
2 teaspoons sake or medium dry sherry
½ teaspoon light brown soft sugar
cornflour, for shaping
soya or sunflower oil, for frying

Dipping sauce:
1 small red pepper, cored, deseeded and finely chopped
1 garlic clove, crushed
125 ml (4 fl oz) sake or dry sherry
125 ml (4 fl oz) light soy sauce
1 tablespoon malt vinegar
1 teaspoon soft brown sugar

To garnish:
thin green pepper strips
thin yellow pepper strips

Mix together the pork, mushrooms, spring onions, beaten egg, fresh breadcrumbs, soy sauce, sake or sherry and sugar. Dust your hands lightly with cornflour and form the mixture into about 18 small balls. Cover and chill in the refrigerator for about 30 minutes.

For the sauce, mix together all the ingredients, blending them well. Pour the dipping sauce into small individual bowls.

Heat a little oil in a frying pan over a moderate heat and fry the pork balls, turning them frequently, until they are evenly cooked and lightly browned. Drain the pork balls on kitchen paper and serve immediately, garnished with strips of green and yellow pepper, with the bowls of dipping sauce.

Serves 4–6

far left: Swedish meat cakes
below: Japanese pork balls with dipping sauce

Indonesian Meatballs

These fragrant spiced meatballs are cooked in coconut milk in the classic Indonesian manner. They will serve four people as a main course or eight as a starter. To ring the changes, you could try using minced lamb instead of beef.

2 onions
500 g (1 lb) lean minced beef
50 g (2 oz) desiccated coconut
2 teaspoons ground coriander
2½ tablespoons oil
1 green pepper, cored, deseeded and diced
1 red chilli, deseeded and diced
175 g (6 oz) long-grain rice
½ teaspoon turmeric
½ teaspoon ground ginger
450 ml (¾ pint) coconut milk
2 tablespoons creamed coconut
2 tablespoons lime juice
To garnish:
1 lime, quartered
coriander leaves
chilli flower (optional)

Finely chop 1 onion and then mix with the minced beef, desiccated coconut, coriander and 1 teaspoon of the oil; add a little water to make the mixture cling together. Form into 32 walnut-sized balls.

Heat the remaining oil in a large pan, add the meatballs in batches and fry until browned, shaking the pan to prevent sticking. Remove the meatballs and pour off all but 2 tablespoons of fat from the pan.

Slice the remaining onion, add to the pan with the green pepper and fry until softened. Add the chilli, rice, turmeric and ground ginger and stir well to coat with oil. Add the coconut milk and the creamed coconut and stir again.

Bring to the boil and return the meatballs to the pan. Cover and simmer gently for 12–15 minutes, until the rice is tender and all the liquid has been absorbed.

Pour the lime juice over the meatballs and rice. Garnish with the lime quarters, fresh coriander leaves and a chilli flower, if using.

Serves 4

Cheesy-topped Burgers

To make healthy low fat burgers, use really lean minced beef or, better still, ground steak. If wished, you could top the burgers with a spoonful of low-fat soft cheese and a sprinkling of herbs.

750 g (1½ lb) lean minced beef
50 g (2 oz) fresh white breadcrumbs
1 teaspoon dried mixed herbs
1 egg, beaten
salt and freshly ground black pepper
Topping:
100 g (3½ oz) full-fat soft cheese
2 tablespoons snipped chives

Put the minced beef, breadcrumbs and herbs in a large mixing bowl and stir well. Season to taste with salt and pepper and then bind the mixture with the beaten egg.

Divide the beef mixture into 4–6 portions and shape each one into a thick burger. Place them under a preheated hot grill and cook for about 8 minutes on each side until well-browned and cooked through. (If the burgers brown too quickly, reduce the heat to moderate.) Alternatively, you can cook the burgers outside over hot coals on a preheated barbecue.

Meanwhile, beat the topping ingredients until soft, adding salt and pepper to taste.

Remove the burgers from the grill. Spoon a portion of the topping mixture on to each one and pop back under the grill to heat through. Serve immediately.

Serves 4–6

right: Indonesian meatballs

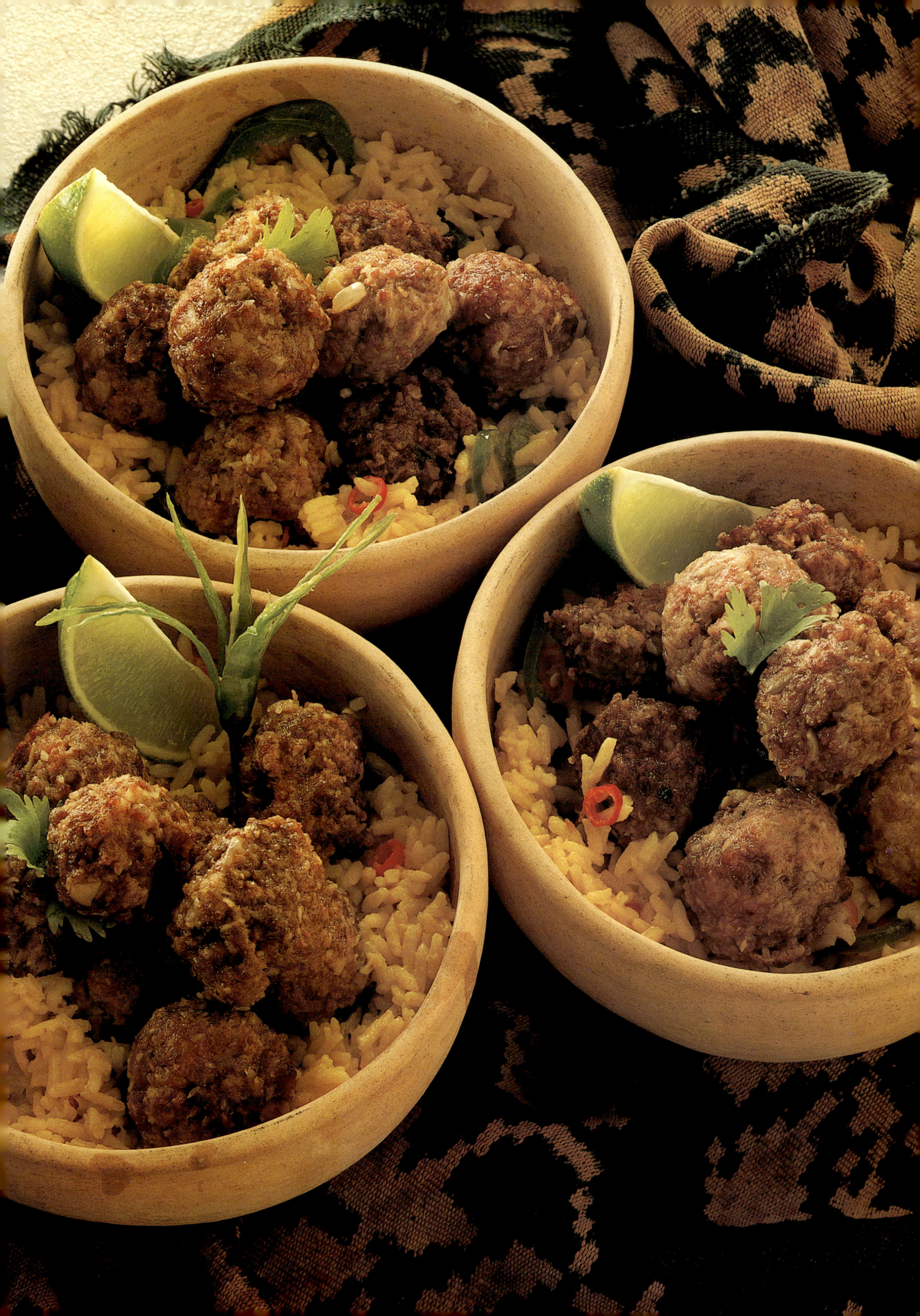

Beef and Peanut Burgers

75 g (3 oz) salted peanuts
500 g (1 lb) lean minced beef
1 onion, chopped
1 egg, beaten
2 tablespoons vegetable oil
salt and pepper
To serve:
4 baps
2 tomatoes, sliced
a few crisp lettuce leaves

Reserve a few peanuts for the garnish and chop the rest. Mix the chopped peanuts with the minced beef, onion and seasoning to taste, then stir in the beaten egg to bind. Divide the mixture into 4 equal portions and shape each one into a flat round burger.

Heat the oil in a frying pan. Add the burgers and cook them over a moderate heat for 10 minutes, turning occasionally, or until lightly browned and cooked through. Alternatively, cook them on a hot barbecue or under an overhead grill.

Meanwhile, warm the baps. Split them in half and place a burger in each one, topped with tomato slices and a few peanuts. Arrange the baps on a bed of lettuce on a serving dish. Serve immediately.

Serves 4

Serving ideas: Serve the burgers with a crisp green salad and thick-cut crisps dressed with blue cheese dressing, accompanied by hamburger relish.

Variation: Use 125 g (4 oz) chopped mushrooms instead of the peanuts.

Tarragon Meatballs with Mushroom Sauce

Serve these tarragon-flavoured beef meatballs on a bed of green tagliatelle with a tomato and onion salad.

500 g (1 lb) lean minced steak or beef
1 onion, grated
75 g (3 oz) fresh breadcrumbs
1 egg, beaten
1 teaspoon dried tarragon
1–2 tablespoons vegetable oil
salt and pepper
Sauce:
175 g (6 oz) mushrooms, finely chopped

300 ml (½ pint) beef or vegetable stock
3 teaspoons cornflour
3 tablespoons milk
1½ tablespoons tomato purée
1½ teaspoons wine or lemon juice
1–2 teaspoons brown sugar
salt and pepper
To garnish:
tomato wedges
sprigs of tarragon

To make the meatballs, place the minced steak or beef, onion, breadcrumbs, beaten egg, tarragon and salt and pepper in a bowl. Mix well together and then shape into 12 meatballs.

Heat the oil in a large frying pan and gently fry the meatballs, turning them to brown evenly. Remove with a slotted spoon and drain thoroughly on kitchen paper.

Make the mushroom sauce. Add the mushrooms to the pan and cook gently until softened. Stir in the stock. Blend the cornflour with the milk and add the tomato purée, wine or lemon juice, sugar and salt and pepper. Add to the pan and heat, stirring, until the mixture comes to the boil. Cover the pan and simmer for 5 minutes. Carefully place the meatballs in the sauce, then cover again and simmer for a further 20–30 minutes.

Transfer the meatballs to a warmed serving dish and spoon the sauce over the top. Garnish with tomato wedges and tarragon sprigs.

Serves 4

Baja California Guacamole Hamburgers

As its name implies, this recipe comes from just below the Mexican border. This version of guacamole differs from the usual ones as it is made with minced onion and tomato, rather than garlic. Make it as fiery as you like – just add 1–2 chopped chillies, if wished.

1 ripe avocado, peeled and stoned
50 g (2 oz) finely chopped onion
1 tablespoon lemon juice
dash of Tabasco sauce
50 g (2 oz) skinned and finely chopped tomatoes
750 g (1½ lb) lean minced beef
salt and pepper
To garnish:
sliced tomatoes
sprigs of parsley

To make the guacamole, mash the avocado with the onion, lemon juice, salt, pepper and Tabasco sauce. Lightly stir in the tomatoes.

Season the minced beef with salt and pepper and shape into 4 thick patties, handling them lightly. Heat a heavy frying pan until very hot and sprinkle lightly with salt – it will instantly begin to brown. Put in the meat and cook over a high heat, turning once, for about 2 minutes on each side for really rare, 6–7 minutes on each side if you like burgers well done.

Put a piece of foil in the bottom of the grill pan. Spoon a little of the guacamole mixture on to each of the hamburgers and then set them under a preheated hot grill and cook for about 1 minute, until the mixture bubbles. Serve at once garnished with sliced tomatoes and parsley sprigs. Serve any remaining guacamole separately.

Serves 4

far left: beef and peanut burgers
above: Baja California guacamole hamburgers

Golden Onionburgers

1 large white onion, peeled
750 g (1½ lb) lean minced beef
1 egg, beaten
1 teaspoon salt
freshly ground black pepper
1 small garlic clove, crushed (optional)
1 teaspoon Worcestershire sauce
1 large bloomer or other long oval-shaped loaf
6 slices tomato
sprigs of parsley, to garnish
To serve:
Snappy Cheese Sauce (see right)

Cut 6 thin slices from the onion and wrap tightly in clingfilm. Finely chop the remaining onion and mix with the minced beef, beaten egg, salt and pepper, garlic (if using) and Worcestershire sauce.

Shape the mixture into 6 oval burgers, about 2 cm (¾ inch) thick. Heat a heavy frying pan until very hot and add the burgers without oil or fat. Cook over a high heat, turning once, according to taste.

While the burgers are cooking, cut 6 thick slices from the loaf and toast them. Top each slice of toast with an onionburger, a slice of tomato and a few onion rings. Pour the hot cheese sauce over the top. Garnish with a sprig of parsley and serve immediately.

Serves 6

Snappy Cheese Sauce

15 g (½ oz) butter
1 tablespoon plain flour
pinch of salt
dash of Tabasco sauce
175 ml (6 fl oz) milk
125 g (4 oz) mature Cheddar cheese, grated
½ teaspoon made mustard

In a heavy saucepan, mix the butter, flour, salt, Tabasco sauce and milk. Cook over a low heat, stirring or beating continuously, until the sauce bubbles and thickens. Continue to cook for 2 more minutes, stirring. Add the grated cheese and cook gently over a low heat until the cheese melts and is just blended. Check the seasoning and stir in the mustard.

Serves 4

Mexican Burgers with Guacamole

750 g (1½ lb) lean minced beef
pinch of ground cumin
pinch of garlic salt
4 spring onions, chopped
freshly ground black pepper
Guacamole:
1 large avocado
3 tablespoons lemon juice
1 garlic clove, crushed
salt and freshly ground black pepper
To garnish:
shredded white cabbage
lemon wedges

Mix together the minced beef, cumin, garlic salt, spring onions and black pepper to taste. Divide the mixture into 4 equal-sized portions and shape each one into a round flat burger. Cover and chill in the refrigerator until needed.

To make the guacamole, cut the avocado in half, discard the stone and scoop out the flesh with a spoon into a bowl. Mash with a fork and mix with the lemon juice, garlic and seasoning. Do this shortly before cooking and serving the burgers. If the guacamole is left too long, it may discolour.

Preheat the grill and cook the burgers for 4–5 minutes on each side, depending on how rare you prefer them. Alternatively, cook them on a hot barbecue.

Arrange the shredded cabbage on a serving dish and place the burgers on top. On each burger, put a spoonful of guacamole and top with a lemon wedge.

Serves 4

soya or sunflower oil, for frying
salt and pepper
To garnish:
lemon slices, peeled and halved
sprigs of rosemary

Combine the veal with the onion. Crush the rosemary leaves and fork them into the mixture. Add the breadcrumbs and milk and beat in one of the eggs. Season with salt and pepper. Form the mixture into small oval meatballs, using a spoon dipped in flour; then set aside in a cool place.

Beat the remaining egg in a bowl. Put the chicken stock, flour, lemon rind and juice in a small saucepan and whisk until smooth. Continue whisking over a moderate heat for about 2 minutes until the sauce thickens. Season to taste with salt and pepper. Bring the sauce to the boil and pour it on to the beaten egg, whisking well until smooth. Remove from the heat and set aside.

Heat the oil in a heavy-based frying pan over a moderate heat. Fry the veal frikadeller, turning them frequently, until they are golden on all sides. Transfer them to a heated serving platter and serve hot, with the egg and lemon sauce spooned over them. Garnish with lemon slices and rosemary sprigs.

Serves 4

---

far left: golden onionburgers with snappy cheese sauce
below: veal and rosemary frikadeller

Veal and Rosemary Frikadeller

500 g (1 lb) lean minced veal
1 small onion, finely chopped
1 tablespoon rosemary leaves
4 tablespoons wholemeal breadcrumbs
150 ml (¼ pint) semi-skimmed milk
2 eggs
300 ml (½ pint) chicken stock
1 tablespoon wholemeal flour
finely grated rind and juice of ½ lemon

Scandinavian Meatballs

250 g (8 oz) minced pork
250 g (8 oz) minced veal
grated nutmeg
50 g (2 oz) butter, softened
50 g (2 oz) white breadcrumbs
2 tablespoons oil
125 g (4 oz) pickled cucumbers, sliced
1 garlic clove, crushed
50 g (2 oz) egg noodles, broken into pieces
1 cauliflower, broken into florets
300 ml (½ pint) chicken stock
150 ml (¼ pint) soured cream
1 teaspoon chopped dill
6–8 pickled baby beets, diced
1 tablespoon vinegar
salt and pepper

Put the minced pork and veal in a basin and season with nutmeg and salt and pepper. Add the butter and breadcrumbs and knead together, adding 1–2 teaspoons water, if necessary. Form into 20 small balls.

Fry the meatballs in the oil until browned. Add the cucumber, garlic, noodles, cauliflower and stock, and season with salt and pepper. Bring to the boil, cover the pan and simmer for 25 minutes. Transfer to a warmed serving dish.

Pour the soured cream on top and sprinkle with dill. Toss the beetroot in the vinegar, drain and pile in the centre.

Serves 4

Danish Frikadeller

500 g (1 lb) minced pork
2 tablespoons plain flour
1 small onion, finely grated
½ teaspoon grated nutmeg or ground allspice
150 ml (¼ pint) milk
25 g (1 oz) butter
4 tablespoons vegetable oil
salt and pepper
sprigs of parsley, to garnish
salad, to serve

Put the minced pork in a bowl and stir in the flour, onion, nutmeg or allspice, salt and plenty of pepper. Gradually add the milk, stirring well to mix. Cover the bowl and leave in the refrigerator or a cool place for at least 1 hour.

Heat the butter and oil in a large heavy-based frying pan. Using a greased tablespoon, take 8 heaped teaspoons of the mince mixture, shape into rounded ovals and add to the pan.

Fry the frikadeller over a low heat for about 12–15 minutes, turning them once, until they are golden and crisp on the outside and cooked right through.

Remove the meatballs from the pan with a slotted spoon and arrange them with the salad on a large serving dish. Garnish with parsley sprigs and serve.

Serves 4

Classic Hamburgers

500 g (1 lb) best-quality lean minced beef
a little fat or oil, for frying
salt and pepper
To serve:
hamburger buns, toasted
tomato relish
lettuce leaves
cheese slices (optional)

Season the minced beef with salt and pepper and form into 6 round flat burgers. If the meat is very lean, you will need to grease the grill pan, barbecue grill or frying pan with a very little fat or oil. If there is a reasonable amount of fat in the meat, this is not necessary. The grill or frying pan should be preheated so that the meat starts to cook the moment it touches the surface.

Grill the hamburgers over hot coals on a barbecue or under a preheated hot grill for 8–10 minutes, turning them once during cooking. Alternatively, you can fry them in a frying pan.

Serve the burgers on toasted hamburger buns with tomato relish, lettuce and cheese slices, if wished.

Makes 6

right: Scandinavian meatballs

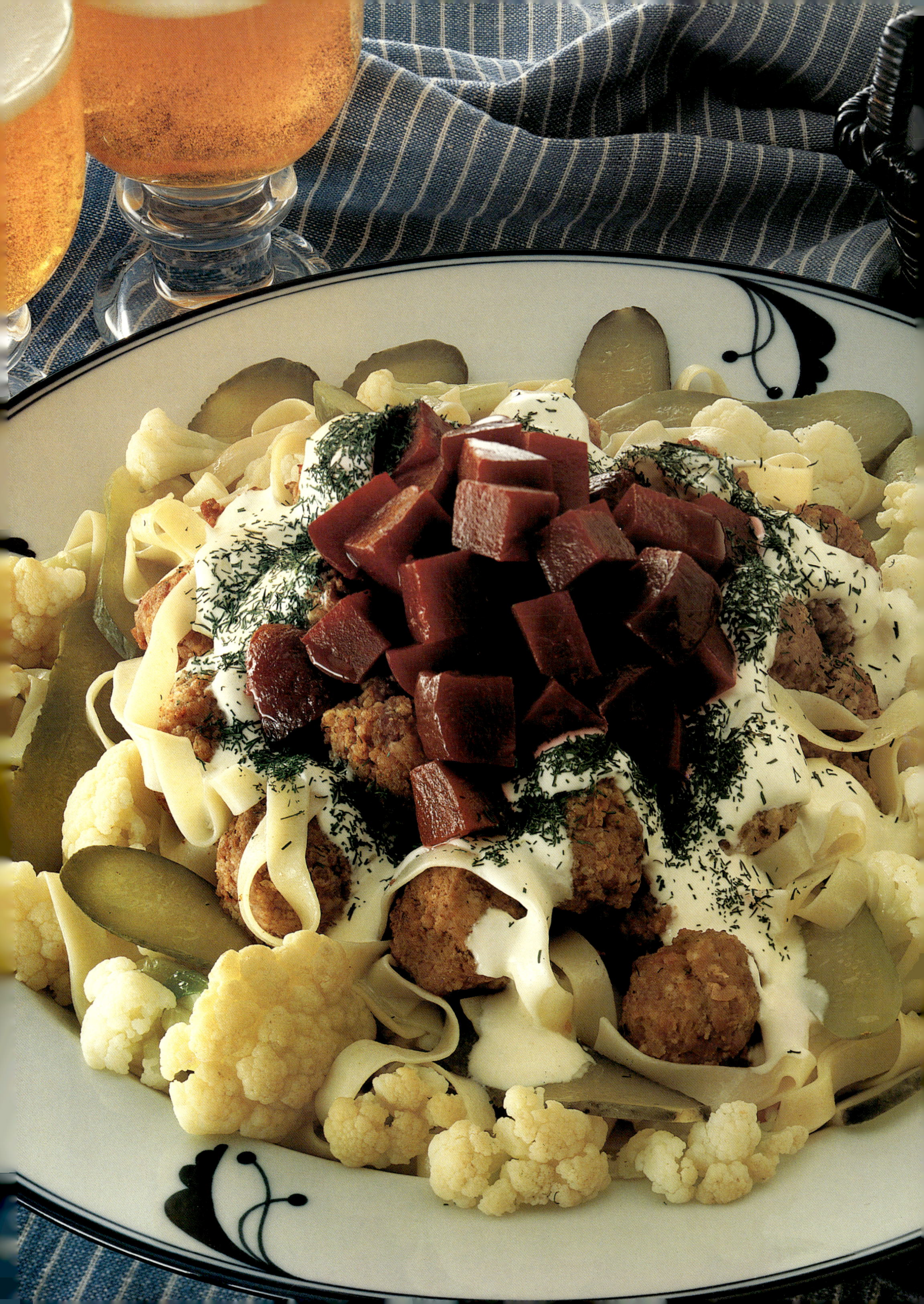

Lamb and Mint Meatballs

500 g (1 lb) minced lamb
2 cloves garlic, crushed
2 teaspoons mint sauce
1 egg, beaten
oil, for shallow frying
salt and pepper
Piquant Dip:
50 g (2 oz) demerara sugar
2 teaspoons cornflour
3 tablespoons water
4 tablespoons redcurrant jelly
2 tablespoons Worcestershire sauce
sprigs of parsley, to garnish

Put the lamb in a bowl and add the garlic and mint sauce. Season well with salt and pepper and bind the mixture with the beaten egg. With floured hands, roll the mixture into walnut-sized balls.

Heat the oil in a frying pan, add the meatballs in batches and fry for about 10 minutes until golden brown. Remove, drain on kitchen paper and keep warm.

To make the dip, put the sugar, cornflour and water in a small pan and blend in the redcurrant jelly and Worcestershire sauce. Bring slowly to the boil and cook, stirring, until smooth.

Spear the meatballs on to cocktail sticks. Garnish with parsley sprigs and serve warm with the dip.

Makes about 25

right: lamb meatballs with apricot sauce
below: lamb and mint meatballs

Lamb Meatballs with Apricot Sauce

750 g (1½ lb) lean minced lamb
finely grated rind of 1 orange
1 garlic clove, crushed
1 teaspoon mixed spice
1 small red pepper, cored, deseeded and finely chopped
25 g (1 oz) raisins, chopped
salt and pepper
2 egg yolks

Marinade:
5 tablespoons orange juice
6 tablespoons olive oil
3 tablespoons red wine

Apricot sauce:
1 small onion, finely chopped
2 tablespoons olive oil
500 g (1 lb) fresh or drained canned apricots, chopped
1 tablespoon chopped mint
150 ml (¼ pint) dry white wine
2 teaspoons clear honey

Mix the minced lamb with the orange rind, garlic, mixed spice, red pepper, raisins and salt and pepper. Beat in the egg yolks. Divide the mixture into 20 equal portions and shape each one into a ball. Put in a shallow dish.

Mix the marinade ingredients together and spoon over the meatballs. Marinate them in the refrigerator, covered, for 4–6 hours, turning them over once or twice.

To make the apricot sauce, fry the chopped onion gently in the olive oil for 2 minutes, then add the remaining ingredients and simmer gently for 10 minutes.

Remove the meatballs from their marinade and drain, reserving the marinade. Take 4 kebab skewers and carefully thread 5 meatballs on to each one. Brush evenly all over with the leftover marinade.

Cook the meatballs on the oiled grill of a preheated barbecue (or under an overhead grill) for 8–10 minutes, turning them once and brushing with the remaining marinade. Serve the meatballs with the hot sauce.

Serves 4

Devilled Meatballs

625 g (1¼ lb) minced beef
40 g (1½ oz) fresh breadcrumbs
1 small onion, finely chopped
1 tablespoon Worcestershire sauce
2 tablespoons oil
250 g (8 oz) carrots, cut into thin sticks
1 large cooking apple, peeled, cored and diced
salt and pepper
chopped parsley, to garnish
Sauce:
1 tablespoon flour
1½ teaspoons dry mustard
1½ teaspoons Dijon mustard
1 tablespoon soy sauce
1 tablespoon Worcestershire sauce
1 tablespoon sweet chutney
300 ml (½ pint) beef stock

Mix the minced beef thoroughly with the breadcrumbs, onion, Worcestershire sauce and seasoning. Divide the mixture into 16 portions and then shape into balls.

Heat the oil in a pan and fry the meatballs gently until browned. Remove from the pan and pour off all but 1 tablespoon of the oil.

To make the sauce, stir the flour and dry mustard into the residue in the pan, followed by the Dijon mustard, soy sauce, Worcestershire sauce, chutney and stock. Bring to the boil and add plenty of salt and pepper to taste.

Arrange the carrots and apples in a casserole dish and then place the meatballs on top. Pour the sauce over and cover the casserole. Cook in a preheated oven, 180°C (350°F), Gas Mark 4, for about 45 minutes.

Uncover the casserole, skim off any fat from the surface and stir lightly. Serve the meatballs hot with spaghetti or noodles, garnished with chopped parsley.

Serves 6

Mu Shu Pork Pockets

The Mu Shu pork is a variant of a traditional Chinese dish, made into an American hamburger form. It is usually served in 'pocket bread' as pittas are called there, with a selection of crisp salad vegetables.

500 g (1 lb) minced pork, or 250 g (8 oz) minced pork mixed with 250 g (8 oz) lean minced beef
1 small onion, finely chopped
75 g (3 oz) canned water chestnuts, drained and coarsely chopped
1 garlic clove, crushed
50 g (2 oz) fine breadcrumbs
1 egg
2 tablespoons soy sauce
½ teaspoon ground ginger
2 tablespoons hoisin sauce (Chinese barbecue sauce)
To serve:
8 pitta breads
6 spring onions, trimmed and cut into matchstick strips
1 large tomato, halved and sliced
soft or crisp lettuce leaves, shredded
finely chopped parsley (optional)

Mix together the minced meat, onion, water chestnuts, garlic, breadcrumbs, egg, soy sauce, ginger and hoisin sauce in a bowl. Shape into flat oval patties.

Heat a wide, heavy frying pan until very hot – do not oil it. Cook the patties over a moderate to high heat for about 8 minutes on each side, turning once, or until the meat shows no pink when it is pierced with a sharp knife.

While the meat is cooking, wrap the pitta breads in foil and warm under a preheated grill. Slit them open and put a meat patty in each one, then tuck in the spring onions, sliced tomato, lettuce leaves and chopped parsley, if liked.

Serves 4

---

right: devilled meatballs

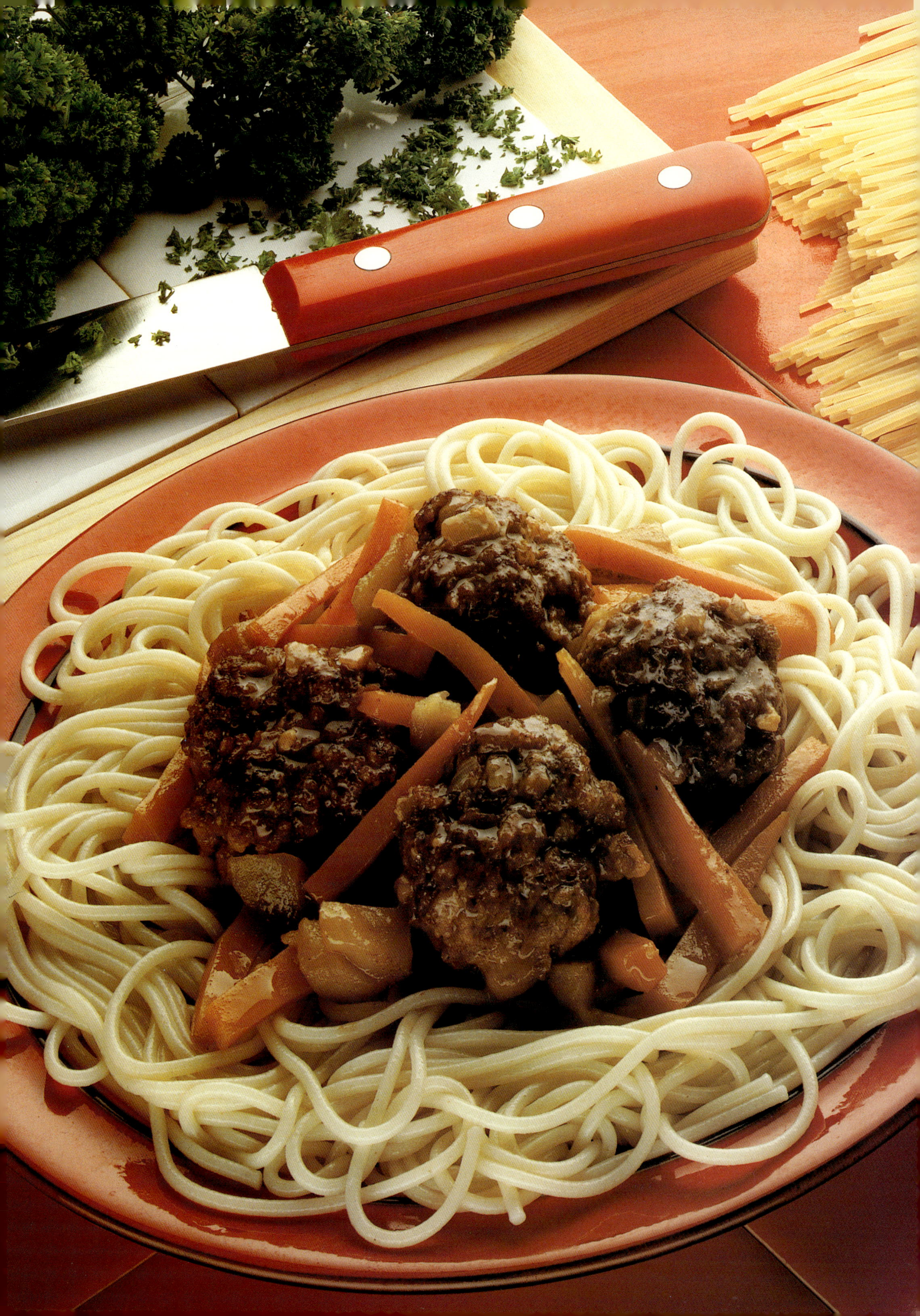

Meatballs in Horseradish Sauce

Horseradish is the traditional partner to beef and this recipe is no exception to the rule. However, if wished, you could try substituting minced pork instead. For the best results, use extra lean ground steak in the meatballs, and real chicken stock in the sauce. Serve with steamed or boiled broccoli.

1 cm (½ inch) thick slice of white bread cut from a large loaf, crusts removed
500 g (1 lb) lean beef, minced twice
¼ teaspoon mustard powder
1 egg, beaten
flour, for shaping
25 g (1 oz) butter
salt and freshly ground black pepper
chopped parsley, to garnish
Sauce:
15 g (½ oz) butter
2 teaspoons plain flour
300 ml (½ pint) chicken stock
2 tablespoons horseradish sauce
½ teaspoon lemon juice
salt and freshly ground black pepper

Soak the bread for a few minutes in water, then squeeze it dry. Mix together the bread and minced beef, mashing it vigorously with a wooden spoon until it forms a paste. Add a little salt and pepper and the mustard powder and beat in the egg. Alternatively, put everything in a food processor and process for a few seconds.

Flour your hands and shape the meat mixture into large balls. Fry them in the butter for about 6–8 minutes, turning them over and over until they are evenly brown and crisp. Remove from the pan, drain on kitchen paper and keep warm while you make the sauce.

To make the sauce, melt the butter in the pan, stir in the flour and then the chicken stock. Bring to the boil, stirring until smooth, and then add the horseradish sauce and lemon juice. Season to taste with salt and pepper.

Return the meatballs to the pan, cover and simmer over a low heat for 3 minutes. Serve hot, garnished with chopped parsley, a green vegetable and new potatoes.

Serves 4

left: meatballs in horseradish sauce

Skewered Meatballs

Throughout Greece, Turkey and the Middle East, minced lamb is flavoured with spices and made into meatballs. In this recipe they are threaded on to skewers with colourful peppers.

500 g (1 lb) lamb fillet, minced
1 onion, finely chopped or grated
2 teaspoons fresh thyme or
   ¼ teaspoon dried
2 garlic cloves, crushed
2 egg yolks
1 large red pepper, cored and deseeded
1 large green pepper, cored and deseeded
5 tablespoons oil
generous pinch of ground ginger
pinch of ground turmeric
salt and pepper
Yogurt and Cucumber Sauce:
½ cucumber, peeled and grated
½ teaspoon dill seed
generous pinch of caster sugar
150 ml (¼ pint) natural yogurt
1 tablespoon chopped mint
salt and pepper

Mix the minced lamb with the onion, thyme, garlic and egg yolks and a little salt and pepper. Form into 24 small meatballs about the size of a chestnut. Cover and chill in the refrigerator for 3–4 hours to firm up the texture of the meatballs.

Cut the red and green peppers into pieces, approximately 2.5 cm (1 inch) square. Thread the prepared meatballs and pieces of pepper alternately on to 4 kebab skewers. Put into a shallow dish.

Mix the oil with the ginger, turmeric and salt and pepper to taste and brush over the prepared kebabs. Cover and chill for 1 hour.

Meanwhile, make the yogurt and cucumber sauce. Squeeze the grated cucumber in a piece of muslin to remove any excess moisture. Mix the cucumber with the dill, sugar, yogurt, mint and salt and pepper.

Arrange the kebabs on the rack of the grill pan and brush lightly with the flavoured oil. Cook under a preheated grill for 6–8 minutes. Turn the kebabs, brushing again with the flavoured oil, and cook for a further 6 minutes. Serve them hot with the yogurt and cucumber sauce and a crisp mixed salad.

Serves 4

Beef and Raisin Meatballs

Another Middle Eastern recipe in which the minced beef is mixed with spices, raisins and walnuts. Instead of grilling, the meatballs are simmered in yogurt.

500 g (1 lb) lean steak, finely minced
1 small onion, finely chopped
2 tablespoons seedless raisins, chopped
2 tablespoons walnuts, chopped
2 tablespoons chopped parsley
¼ teaspoon ground allspice
¼ teaspoon ground cumin
1 egg, beaten
flour, for shaping
salt and freshly ground black pepper
sprigs of mint, to garnish
boiled rice, to serve
Sauce:
300 ml (½ pint) natural yogurt
1 teaspoon lemon juice

Blend the steak in a blender or food processor until it is a smooth paste. Beat in the onion, raisins, walnuts, parsley and allspice. Season with salt and pepper and beat in just enough of the egg to bind the mixture to a firm paste.

Flour your hands and shape the mixture into rounds almost the size of golf balls. Place the meatballs in a single layer in a large flameproof casserole and pour the yogurt and lemon juice over the top. Season lightly with salt and pepper.

Cover the casserole and simmer gently over a low heat for 45 minutes until the meatballs are cooked. Garnish with mint sprigs and serve with plain boiled rice.

Serves 4

left: chillied meatballs
right: Italian porkballs

Chillied Meatballs

1 small onion, finely chopped
500 g (1 lb) lean minced beef
40 g (1½ oz) wholemeal breadcrumbs
2 teaspoons chilli powder
1 teaspoon finely grated lemon rind
1 egg, beaten
wholemeal flour, for shaping
1 green pepper, cored, deseeded and sliced
1 teaspoon soya or sunflower oil
250 g (8 oz) can chopped tomatoes
1 teaspoon soft brown sugar
150 ml (¼ pint) beef stock
freshly ground black pepper
sprigs of parsley, to garnish
boiled rice or jacket potatoes, to serve

In a bowl, combine the onion with the minced beef, breadcrumbs, chilli powder, lemon rind, egg and black pepper to taste. Mix thoroughly and, with lightly floured hands, divide the mixture into 12 and form into small balls. Place them in the refrigerator to chill while making the sauce.

In a large pan, sauté the green pepper in the oil for 2 minutes to soften it. Add the tomatoes, sugar and stock. Bring the sauce to the boil and add the meatballs. Cover the pan and simmer for 15 minutes, turning the meatballs once. Garnish with parsley sprigs and serve hot with boiled rice or jacket potatoes.

Serves 4

Italian Porkballs

750 g (1½ lb) minced pork
2 garlic cloves, crushed
½ teaspoon ground cinnamon
good pinch of ground cloves
1 egg, beaten
25 g (1 oz) flour
3 tablespoons oil
1 large onion, chopped
1 red pepper, cored, deseeded and sliced
6 tomatoes, skinned and sliced
1 tablespoon tomato purée
6 whole cloves
150 ml (¼ pint) red wine
1 tablespoon cornflour
salt and freshly ground black pepper
cooked pasta, to serve (optional)

Combine the minced pork with 1 garlic clove, the cinnamon, cloves and salt and pepper. Bind with the beaten egg and divide into 16 equal-sized portions. Shape into balls and then roll in the flour.

Heat the oil and fry the porkballs until lightly browned all over, turning them frequently. Transfer to an ovenproof casserole dish.

Fry the onion and remaining garlic in the same pan until soft. Add the red pepper and cook until the onions are lightly browned. Add the tomatoes, tomato purée, cloves, wine and seasoning to taste and pour over the porkballs.

Cover and cook in a preheated oven at 180°C (350°F), Gas Mark 4, for 50–60 minutes. Discard the cloves and skim away any fat. Blend the cornflour with a little cold water and stir into the sauce. Bring to the boil, stirring until thickened and smooth, and check the seasoning. Serve on a bed of pasta, if liked.

Serves 4

Guinness Meat Loaf

This meat loaf has a rich, slightly bitter flavour from the Guinness. A sweet stout or even a medium dry cider could be substituted if preferred.

125 g (4 oz) fresh white breadcrumbs
200 ml (7 fl oz) Guinness
375 g (12 oz) minced beef
375 g (12 oz) minced pork
1 small onion, finely chopped
1 tablespoon chopped fresh rosemary
1 egg, beaten
pinch of freshly grated nutmeg
125 g (4 oz) Edam cheese, diced
salt and freshly ground black pepper

Grease and line a 1 kg (2 lb) loaf tin. Put the breadcrumbs in a bowl with the Guinness. Leave for 30 minutes.

Mix the minced meats in a bowl with the onion, rosemary, beaten egg, salt, pepper and nutmeg. Add the Guinness-soaked breadcrumbs and mix thoroughly together.

Stir the Edam into the meat mixture and then spoon into the prepared loaf tin, smoothing the surface level. Cover the meat loaf with a piece of greased kitchen foil.

Cook in a preheated oven, 180°C (350°F), Gas Mark 4, for 1½ hours. Peel back the foil and carefully drain away any excess juices from the tin. Leave the meat loaf until it is completely cold before slicing.

Serves 6

Meat Loaf

Meat loaves are very versatile as you can serve them hot for an easy, economical family meal, or leave to go cold and then serve sliced for a picnic or for a casual supper.

500 g (1 lb) lean minced beef
125 g (4 oz) pork sausagemeat
125 g (4 oz) fresh breadcrumbs
1 onion, finely chopped
½ tablespoon Worcestershire sauce
1 tablespoon tomato ketchup
½ teaspoon dried mixed herbs
2 teaspoons finely chopped parsley
1 teaspoon made mustard
salt and freshly ground black pepper
2 eggs, beaten
To garnish:
crisp lettuce leaves
tomato slices
cucumber slices
sprigs of parsley

Place all the ingredients, except the beaten eggs, in a bowl and then mix together. Bind the mixture with the beaten egg.

Pack the meat loaf mixture into a 1 kg (2 lb) loaf tin and cover with foil. Bake in a preheated oven, 190°C (375°F), Gas Mark 5, for 1 hour or until cooked through.

Loosen the sides of the loaf with a knife, then turn out on to a warmed serving dish. Garnish with lettuce, tomato, cucumber slices and parsley.

Serves 6

Variation: Spoon half of the meat mixture into the tin, then spread 125 g (4 oz) curd cheese over the top. Cover with the remaining mixture.

Meat Loaf with Spinach

This meatloaf looks particularly pretty as the tin is lined with fresh spinach leaves. A fresh tomato sauce would make an excellent accompaniment. Just sauté some chopped onion and garlic in oil, add chopped canned or fresh tomatoes and cook gently until thick and pulpy. Season with salt and pepper and some chopped fresh basil leaves.

250 g (8 oz) fresh spinach, tough stalks removed
375 g (12 oz) lean minced beef
250 g (8 oz) low fat sausages, skinned
75 g (3 oz) dry country stuffing mix
75 ml (3 fl oz) cold water
200 g (7 oz) can sweetcorn, drained
1 egg, beaten
To garnish:
tomato slices
spring onions

Lightly oil a 1 kg (2 lb) loaf tin. Wash the spinach leaves in several changes of cold water. Place them in a pan with just the water clinging to the leaves. Cover tightly with a lid and cook for 2 minutes or until the leaves have wilted, shaking the pan occasionally. Drain, keeping the leaves whole. Use the leaves to line the base and sides of the loaf tin.

Combine the minced beef with the sausagemeat. Place the stuffing mix in a bowl, pour over the water and stir well. Add the stuffing to the meats with the sweetcorn and egg, and mix everything together. Spoon the mixture into the spinach-lined tin, pressing it down firmly and smoothing the top.

Place the tin in a preheated oven, 180°C (350°F), Gas Mark 4, and bake the loaf for 1¼ hours or until the juices run clear. Leave the cooked loaf to cool in the tin for a few minutes before turning out. Serve hot or cold, garnished with tomato slices and spring onions.

Serves 6

right: meat loaf

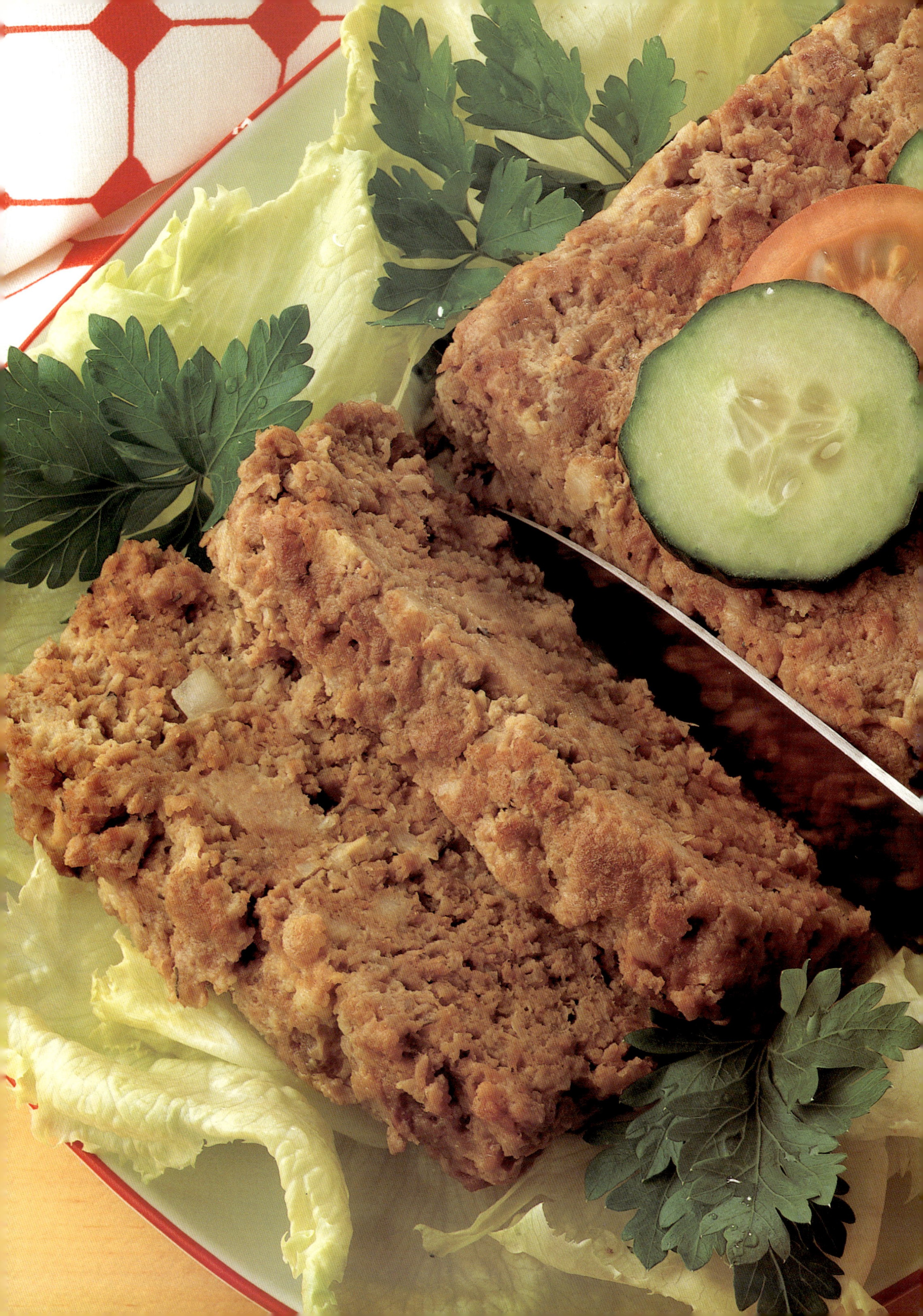

Turkey and Broccoli Loaf

50 g (2 oz) button mushrooms, sliced
15 g (½ oz) butter
250 g (8 oz) turkey breast meat, minced
250 g (8 oz) dark turkey meat, minced
1 onion, grated
50 g (2 oz) fresh breadcrumbs
2 small eggs, beaten
2 tablespoons double cream
pinch of dried tarragon
125 g (4 oz) broccoli florets, lightly cooked
salt and freshly ground black pepper

Sauce (optional):
15 g (½ oz) butter
50 g (2 oz) mushrooms, chopped
15 g (½ oz) plain flour
150 ml (¼ pint) chicken stock
150 ml (¼ pint) milk

To garnish:
salad leaves
tomatoes
boiled new potatoes, to serve (optional)

Lightly fry the mushrooms in the butter and then arrange them in an overlapping line down the centre of a well-greased 500 g (1 lb) loaf tin.

In a large bowl, mix together the turkey, onion, breadcrumbs, eggs, cream, tarragon and some salt and pepper to taste.

Put half of the mixture into the loaf tin. Cover with the broccoli florets, then top with the remaining turkey mixture. Cover with foil and place in a roasting tin filled with boiling water. Cook in a preheated oven, 180°C (350°F), Gas Mark 4, for 1¼–1½ hours.

Meanwhile, make the sauce (if serving). Melt the butter in a pan, add the mushrooms and fry lightly. Stir in the flour and cook for 2–3 minutes. Add the stock and milk gradually, stirring all the time, and then season to taste with salt and pepper. Bring to the boil and cook for 2–3 minutes, stirring constantly.

When the loaf is cooked, turn it out of the tin, garnish with salad leaves and tomatoes and serve sliced with the mushroom sauce and new potatoes, if liked.

Serves 4

above left: turkey and broccoli loaf
right: stuffed veal loaf

Stuffed Veal Loaf

4 eggs
4 veal escalopes
500 g (1 lb) lean minced veal
75 g (3 oz) fresh wholemeal breadcrumbs
juice and finely grated rind of ½ lemon
1 onion, chopped
2 tablespoons chopped sage
salt and pepper
sage leaves, to garnish

Boil 3 of the eggs for 5 minutes. Set aside to cool and then remove the shells. Place the veal escalopes between 2 sheets of greaseproof paper and beat with a rolling pin until thin and even. Use them to line the base and sides of a 1.25 kg (2½ lb) loaf tin, leaving enough to use as a 'lid'.

Mix together the minced veal, breadcrumbs, lemon juice and rind, onion and sage. Season with salt and pepper. Beat the remaining egg with a fork and stir it into the mixture, mixing well to bind.

Spoon half of the mixture into the veal-lined tin and press it down evenly. Arrange the shelled hard-boiled eggs down the centre and then cover with the remaining meat mixture. Press down evenly and cover with the remaining veal escalope to make a 'lid'. Stand the tin in a roasting tin which has been half-filled with water.

Cook in a preheated oven, 190°C (375°F), Gas Mark 5, for about 1¾ hours until the loaf is thoroughly cooked. Leave the loaf to cool in the tin, then turn out and serve sliced, garnished with sage leaves.

Serves 6

Baked in the Oven

Beef Gougère

For a gougère, some choux pastry is piped or spooned into a circle in an ovenproof dish. The filling is turned into the centre of the ring and the dish is then baked in the oven until the choux pastry is risen, crisp and golden brown.

1 large onion, chopped
2 tablespoons oil
500 g (1 lb) lean minced beef
125 g (4 oz) button mushrooms, sliced
425 g (14 oz) can chopped tomatoes
salt and freshly ground black pepper
Choux pastry:
150 ml (¼ pint) water
65 g (2½ oz) butter
65 g (2½ oz) plain flour
2 eggs
125 g (4 oz) grated mature Cheddar cheese
salt and freshly ground black pepper
Topping:
125 g (4 oz) rindless streaky bacon, chopped
25 g (1 oz) grated Cheddar cheese
25 g (1 oz) fresh breadcrumbs

Grease a 25 cm (10 inch) deep ovenproof dish. Fry the onion in the oil until softened but not browned. Add the minced beef and cook, breaking it up as it cooks, until evenly browned. Stir in the mushrooms and cook for a few minutes, then season with salt and pepper and pour in the tomatoes. Bring to the boil, then remove from the heat and set aside.

Pour the water for the choux pastry into a saucepan. Add the butter and heat gently until it melts, then bring to the boil. As soon as the mixture boils, remove the pan from the heat and tip in all the flour. Beat it in well but do not over-mix it; the mixture should come away from the sides of the saucepan in one lump.

Allow to cool for a few minutes. Lightly beat the eggs, then beat them vigorously into the flour and water paste. Continue beating until the paste is smooth and very glossy. Beat in the grated cheese and season with salt and pepper.

Spoon the choux paste around the edge of the prepared dish, making it as even as possible and piling it up slightly. Pile the minced beef mixture into the middle of the choux pastry ring.

For the topping, mix together the bacon, cheese and breadcrumbs. Scatter over the beef mixture and bake the gougère in a hot preheated oven, 220°C (425°F), Gas Mark 7, for 45 minutes or until the choux pastry is well risen and golden brown. When cut, the pastry will be deliciously moist in the middle.

Serves 4

Beef and Cabbage Cobbler

2 tablespoons oil
1 large onion, chopped
500 g (1 lb) lean minced beef
1 tablespoon fennel seeds or caraway seeds
125 g (4 oz) carrots, cut into thin strips
125 g (4 oz) button mushrooms, sliced
600 ml (1 pint) pale ale
1 beef stock cube
500 g (1 lb) white cabbage, shredded
salt and pepper

Scone Topping:
125 g (4 oz) self-raising flour, plus extra for dusting
pinch of salt
25 g (1 oz) butter
65 ml (2½ fl oz) milk
25 g (1 oz) grated Cheddar cheese

Heat the oil in a large saucepan and then add the onion and fry until soft but not browned. Add the minced beef and cook, breaking up the meat with a wooden spoon, until evenly browned. Stir in the fennel or caraway seeds and cook for 2 minutes, and then add the vegetables and season to taste.

Pour in the ale and crumble in the stock cube, then bring to the boil. Lastly, stir in the cabbage and bring back to the boil. Remove the pan from the heat and transfer the beef mixture to an ovenproof dish.

For the topping, sift the flour into a bowl and add a pinch of salt. Rub in the butter until the mixture resembles fine breadcrumbs, and then stir in the milk to make a soft mixture (it should be softer than a normal scone dough).

Divide the dough into 6 equal portions and roll each one in a little flour. Flatten each piece of dough slightly and then place them on top of the beef mixture.

Sprinkle the grated cheese over the scones and bake in a preheated hot oven, 220°C (425°F), Gas Mark 7, for 25 minutes or until the scones are risen and golden. Serve the hot cobbler immediately.

Serves 4

far left: beef gougère
above: beef and cabbage cobbler

Beef, Okra and Pepper Mould

500 g (1 lb) fresh okra, trimmed
2 tablespoons soya or sunflower oil
1 onion, chopped
500 g (1 lb) lean minced beef
1 garlic clove, crushed
4 tablespoons tomato purée
1½ teaspoons ground coriander
1 red pepper, cored, deseeded and chopped
25 g (1 oz) wholemeal fresh breadcrumbs
300 ml (½ pint) beef stock
salt and pepper
coriander leaves, to garnish

Fry the okra in 1 tablespoon of oil for 3–4 minutes, stirring. Remove from the pan and drain well on kitchen paper. Wipe out the pan and add the remaining oil. Fry the onion for 2 minutes, stirring, and then add the minced beef and stir-fry over a moderate heat until it is evenly coloured.

Add the garlic, tomato purée, ground coriander, red pepper and breadcrumbs, and season with salt and pepper. Stir well to mix.

Arrange half of the okra in the base of a deep 20 cm (8 inch) round cake tin or ovenproof dish, the points radiating outwards from the centre. Spoon half of the beef mixture over the top, then add the remaining okra and cover with the rest of the beef mixture, packing it down evenly. Pour over the stock.

Cover the tin with kitchen foil and bake in a preheated oven, 180°C (350°F), Gas Mark 4, for about 1 hour. Turn out carefully on to a flat serving plate and serve hot, garnished with coriander leaves.

Serves 4

above: beef, okra and pepper mould
right: Angostura mince cobbler

Angostura Mince Cobbler

625 g (1¼ lb) lean minced beef
1 large onion, sliced
2 carrots, diced
300 ml (½ pint) beef stock
1½ tablespoons Angostura bitters
1 tablespoon tomato purée
2 teaspoons cornflour
salt and freshly ground black pepper
Scone topping:
175 g (6 oz) self-raising flour
40 g (1½ oz) butter or margarine
½ teaspoon dried mixed herbs
1 egg, beaten
about 2 tablespoons milk
few sesame seeds (optional)
salt and freshly ground black pepper

Dry-fry the minced beef gently in a pan with no extra fat until the juices begin to run, stirring the beef frequently. Add the onion and carrots and continue cooking for a few more minutes.

Add the stock, Angostura bitters, tomato purée and salt and pepper and bring to the boil. Meanwhile, blend the cornflour with a little cold water, add to the pan and cook, stirring, until thickened.

Transfer the beef mixture to a casserole dish, cover and then cook in a preheated oven, 180°C (350°F), Gas Mark 4, for 20 minutes.

For the scone topping, sift the flour into a bowl and rub in the fat until the mixture resembles fine breadcrumbs. Season with salt and pepper and stir in the herbs. Bind together with the beaten egg and sufficient milk to give a softish dough. Pat out the scone dough on a floured surface to a thickness of about 1 cm (½ inch) and then cut into 4 cm (1½ inch) rounds.

Remove the casserole from the oven and increase the oven temperature to 200°C (400°F), Gas Mark 6. Arrange the scones in an overlapping circle around the top of the casserole. Brush lightly with milk and sprinkle with the sesame seeds (if using).

Return the casserole to the oven and bake, uncovered, for about 20 minutes or until the scones are well risen and golden brown. Serve the cobbler at once.

Serves 4–6

Texan Cobbler

1 teaspoon vegetable oil
1 small onion, finely chopped
250 g (8 oz) lean minced beef
2 x 425 g (14 oz) cans chilli beans
few drops of Tabasco sauce or some dried crushed chillies (optional)
175 g (6 oz) packet scone mix
pinch of cayenne pepper
4 tablespoons beer or water
50 g (2 oz) Cheddar cheese, finely grated
To serve:
shredded lettuce
sliced tomatoes
4 tablespoons soured cream or natural yogurt

Heat the oil in a small frying pan and fry the onion until softened but not brown. Add the minced beef and fry until browned and crumbly. Remove from the heat and drain off any excess fat.

Add the drained chilli beans to the beef with some Tabasco sauce or dried crushed chillies to taste, if liked. Stir to blend, then spoon into a 1.8 litre (3 pint) baking dish.

Mix together the scone mix, cayenne pepper, beer or water and half of the grated cheese. Shape into 6–8 small rounds and place around the edge of the dish. Sprinkle with the remaining cheese.

Bake in a preheated oven, 200°C (400°F), Gas Mark 6, for 20–25 minutes until well risen and golden. Serve the cobbler immediately with some lettuce, tomatoes and soured cream or yogurt.

Serves 4

Kheema Do Pyaza

500 g (1 lb) onions
4 tablespoons oil
2.5 cm (1 inch) piece of fresh root ginger, peeled and chopped
1 garlic clove, finely chopped
2 green chillies, finely chopped
1 teaspoon turmeric
1 teaspoon ground coriander seeds
1 teaspoon ground cumin seeds
750 g (1½ lb) minced lamb
150 ml (¼ pint) natural yogurt
250 g (8 oz) can tomatoes
salt
boiled rice, to serve

Finely chop 375 g (12 oz) onions and then thinly slice the remainder. Heat 2 tablespoons of the oil in a flameproof casserole, add the chopped onions and then fry until golden. Add the ginger, garlic, chillies and spices and fry for about 2 minutes. Add the minced lamb and cook, stirring to break it up, until well browned.

Stir in the yogurt, a spoonful at a time, until it is absorbed, then add the tomatoes with their juice and salt to taste. Bring to the boil, stir well and remove from the heat.

Cover the casserole and cook in a preheated oven, 160°C (325°F), Gas Mark 3, for about 20 minutes until the meat is cooked.

Meanwhile, fry the sliced onions in the remaining oil until brown and crisp. Transfer the meat mixture to a warmed serving dish and sprinkle with the fried onions. Serve immediately with some boiled rice.

Serves 4

Gingered Beef Patties

500 g (1 lb) lean minced beef
1 onion, finely chopped
50 g (2 oz) fresh breadcrumbs
1 egg, beaten
2 tablespoons chopped parsley
2 tablespoons vegetable oil
300 ml (½ pint) boiling beef stock
1 tablespoon dark brown sugar
1 teaspoon ground ginger
50 g (2 oz) raisins
50 ml (2 fl oz) lemon juice
25 g (1 oz) butter
8 pineapple rings, fresh or canned
2 teaspoons arrowroot
2 tablespoons cold water
salt and freshly ground black pepper
To garnish:
4 pieces stem ginger, sliced
sprigs of parsley

Place the minced beef, onion, breadcrumbs, egg and parsley in a large mixing bowl and mix well together. Season with salt and pepper and divide into 8 equal portions. Shape into patties.

Heat the oil in a frying pan, add the patties and fry over a moderate heat for about 5 minutes, turning occasionally, until well browned. Transfer the patties to a flameproof casserole dish.

In a bowl, mix the stock, sugar, ginger, raisins and lemon juice together, then pour over the patties. Cover the casserole dish and cook in a preheated oven, 180°C (350°F), Gas Mark 4, for 45 minutes or until the patties are tender.

Melt the butter in the frying pan, add the pineapple rings and fry over a moderate heat for 2–3 minutes, turning once, until lightly browned on both sides. Transfer to a heated serving dish.

Remove the patties from the casserole and place one on each pineapple ring. Keep warm while you finish off the sauce.

Dissolve the arrowroot in the water and stir into the sauce in the casserole. Bring to the boil, stirring. Adjust the seasoning to taste, then pour the sauce over the patties. Serve at once, garnished with sliced ginger and parsley sprigs.

Serves 4

far left: Texan cobbler
below: gingered beef patties

Tipsy Lamb with Courgettes

This is a simple dish of minced lamb cooked in wine (or stock if preferred) and topped with lightly fried courgettes. Serve with minted new potatoes.

50 g (2 oz) butter
2 celery sticks, cut into rounds
1 onion, halved and thinly sliced
500 g (1 lb) lean minced lamb
2 tablespoons plain flour
450 ml (¾ pint) red wine
2 sprigs rosemary
250 g (8 oz) mushrooms, sliced
375 g (12 oz) courgettes, cut into fine strips
a little lemon juice
2 tablespoons chopped parsley
salt and pepper

Melt half of the butter in a large flameproof casserole and fry the celery and onion. When the onion is just softened, add the minced lamb and some salt and pepper. Continue cooking until the meat is lightly browned, stirring to break it up and ensure that it cooks evenly.

Stir in the flour, then pour in the wine. Add the rosemary and bring to the boil. Remove from the heat. Cover the casserole and cook in a preheated oven, 180°C (350°F), Gas Mark 4, for 20 minutes. Stir in the mushrooms after 15 minutes.

Melt the remaining butter in a pan and fry the courgettes quickly, stirring all the time, until they are very lightly cooked – this should take only a few minutes. Season to taste with some salt and pepper and a little lemon juice, and then stir in the parsley. Transfer the lamb mixture to a serving dish and then arrange the fried courgettes on top. Serve immediately.

Serves 4

below: tipsy lamb with courgettes
right: lamb with flageolet beans

Lamb with Flageolet Beans

Pale green flageolet beans are available in cans as well as dried. Serve this dish with a salad of shredded lettuce, chopped spring onions and croûtons.

375 g (12 oz) dried flageolet beans
1 tablespoon oil
1 large onion, chopped
1 large garlic clove, crushed
500 g (1 lb) lean minced lamb
1 bay leaf
1 tablespoon tarragon
900 ml (1½ pints) chicken stock
250 g (8 oz) mushrooms, sliced
2 tablespoons chopped parsley
salt and pepper
soured cream, to serve

Soak the flageolet beans for several hours or, preferably, overnight in plenty of cold water. The following day, drain them and pick out any bad ones.

Heat the oil in a large heavy-based flameproof casserole. Add the onion and garlic and cook until the onion is softened but not browned. Add the lamb and fry it, stirring all the time, until lightly browned. Stir in the bay leaf, tarragon and plenty of seasoning. Pour in the chicken stock, and then add the beans and bring to the boil.

Reduce the heat and cover the casserole tightly. Transfer to a preheated oven, 180°C (350°F), Gas Mark 4, and cook for about 50–60 minutes. If it is simmering quite gently there should be enough liquid to complete the cooking but it's a good idea to check it about two-thirds of the way through the cooking time.

Stir the mushrooms into the casserole about 5 minutes before the end of the cooking time. When the dish is ready, there should be virtually no cooking liquid left, but the mixture should be moist. Quickly stir in the parsley and serve with a bowl of soured cream.

Serves 4

Beef and Vegetable Kheema

4 tablespoons oil
2 onions, chopped
2 teaspoons ground coriander
½ teaspoon turmeric
2.5 cm (1 inch) piece of fresh root ginger, finely chopped
1 heaped teaspoon garam masala
500 g (1 lb) lean minced beef
250 g (8 oz) small potatoes, quartered
500 g (1 lb) shelled peas

Heat the oil in a flameproof casserole, add the onions and cook until soft. Add the spices and fry for 5 minutes over a low heat. Stir in the minced beef and cook over a high heat until well browned.

Lower the heat and then add the potatoes and salt to taste. Cover and cook gently for 5 minutes, then add the peas. Cover and cook in a preheated oven, 180°C (350°F), Gas Mark 4, for 20–30 minutes until the peas and potatoes are tender. Serve hot with boiled rice.

Serves 4

Moussaka

1 kg (2 lb) aubergines
150 ml (¼ pint) olive oil or cooking oil, for frying
75 g (3 oz) Kefalotyr or Parmesan cheese, grated
3 tablespoons crisp dry breadcrumbs
salt

Meat filling:
1 large onion, finely chopped
2 tablespoons olive or cooking oil
500 g (1 lb) lean minced lamb
500 g (1 lb) tomatoes, roughly chopped
2 tablespoons tomato purée
150 ml (¼ pint) dry white wine
1 tablespoon chopped fresh oregano or fresh basil

large pinch of ground nutmeg
large pinch of ground cinnamon
salt and freshly ground black pepper
75 g (3 oz) Kefalotyri or Parmesan cheese, grated

Sauce:
600 ml (1 pint) milk
small piece of cinnamon stick
1 bay leaf
50 g (2 oz) butter
50 g (2 oz) plain flour

Trim off the ends of the aubergines and discard. Cut the aubergines into 5 mm (¼ inch) slices and place them in a large bowl of well-salted water. Leave to stand for 30 minutes.

Squeeze the aubergine slices gently, then rinse in cold running water; squeeze them again and leave in a colander lined with a tea-towel for 1 hour.

Meanwhile, make the meat filling. Fry the onion gently in the oil for 2–3 minutes. Add the lamb and cook until lightly browned. Add the tomatoes, tomato purée, wine, oregano or basil, nutmeg, cinnamon and salt and pepper. Simmer gently for 30 minutes. Stir the cheese into the meat filling.

Shallow-fry the drained aubergine slices in the oil on both sides until lightly golden. You will probably need to do this in about 3 batches. Remove from the pan and drain thoroughly on kitchen paper.

Spoon half of the meat filling into a large, lightly oiled gratin dish, and lay half of the fried aubergine slices on top. Add the remaining meat filling, then cover with the remaining aubergine slices.

To make the sauce, heat the milk in a pan with the cinnamon stick and bay leaf, then strain. Heat the butter in a pan and stir in the flour. Gradually stir in the strained milk, beating well. Simmer gently without stirring for 2–3 minutes.

Spoon the sauce evenly over the moussaka and sprinkle with the cheese and breadcrumbs. Bake in a preheated oven, 180°C (350°F), Gas Mark 4, for 1 hour until the top of the moussaka is crisp and golden. Serve piping hot with a crisp salad.

Serves 6

Beef and Bean Moussaka

2 aubergines, trimmed and sliced
500 g (1 lb) lean minced beef
1 large onion, thinly sliced
1 garlic clove, crushed
425 g (14 oz) can chopped tomatoes
425 g (14 oz) can red kidney beans, drained
2 tablespoons chopped parsley
2 eggs
300 ml (½ pint) natural Greek yogurt
2 tablespoons finely grated Parmesan cheese
grated nutmeg (optional)
salt and pepper

Arrange the aubergine slices in a colander and sprinkle salt between the layers. Leave to drain for about 30 minutes. Rinse in cold water and then pat dry with kitchen paper.

In a non-stick pan, gently fry the aubergines without fat for 2–3 minutes until they are lightly coloured, turning once. Remove the aubergines and set aside. Fry the minced beef in the pan without any added fat, stirring occasionally, until evenly coloured.

Add the onion and garlic and fry gently over a moderate heat for 2–3 minutes. Stir in the tomatoes, kidney beans and parsley. Bring to the boil, cover the pan and then simmer for 5 minutes.

Arrange alternate layers of the fried aubergine slices and the meat mixture in a 2.5 litre (4 pint) ovenproof dish, starting and finishing with a layer of aubergines.

Beat together the eggs and yogurt, season with a little pepper and pour over the aubergines and meat. Sprinkle with Parmesan and a little grated nutmeg, if using.

Bake the moussaka in a preheated oven, 190°C (375°F), Gas Mark 5, for 35–40 minutes or until golden brown and bubbling.

Serves 4–6

far left: moussaka

Kofta Curry

3 onions, sliced
2 garlic cloves
2 green chillies
3.5 cm (1½ inch) piece of fresh root ginger, peeled
25 g (1 oz) fresh coriander leaves
25 g (1 oz) fresh mint leaves
2 teaspoons salt
500 g (1 lb) lean minced beef
4 tablespoons oil
1 teaspoon chilli powder
1 teaspoon ground cumin
1 tablespoon ground coriander
6 curry leaves
25 g (1 oz) tomato purée, diluted in 300 ml (½ pint) water
sprigs of mint, to garnish

Place 1 onion, 1 garlic clove, the green chillies, one-third of the ginger, the coriander leaves, mint and half of the salt in a food processor or liquidizer and work to a thick, smooth paste.

Mix with the minced beef and roll into walnut-sized balls. Fry lightly in 3 tablespoons of the oil until golden brown and cooked through. Drain the meatballs on kitchen paper and set aside.

Heat the remaining oil in a flameproof casserole, add the rest of the onions and fry until golden. Crush the remaining garlic and chop the rest of the ginger. Add to the casserole with the chilli powder, cumin, ground coriander and 1 tablespoon water. Fry, stirring, for 2 minutes. Add the curry leaves and fry for 30 seconds, and then stir in the diluted tomato purée and the remaining salt.

Simmer for 10 minutes. Slip the meatballs into the casserole, cover and cook in a preheated oven, 180°C (350°F), Gas Mark 4, for 30 minutes. Serve the curry garnished with mint sprigs.

Serves 4

Aubergine Cutlets

2 large aubergines
3 tablespoons oil
1 onion, finely chopped
2 garlic cloves, crushed
2 green chillies, deseeded and finely chopped
1 teaspoon turmeric
500 g (1 lb) lean minced beef
1 egg, lightly beaten
2–3 tablespoons fresh breadcrumbs
salt

Cook the aubergines in boiling salted water for 15 minutes, or until almost tender. Drain thoroughly and set aside to cool.

Heat the oil in a pan, add the onion and fry until golden. Add the garlic, chillies and turmeric and fry for 2 minutes. Add the minced beef and cook, stirring, until brown all over. Add some salt to taste and cook gently for 20 minutes until the meat is tender.

Cut the aubergines in half lengthways. Carefully scoop out the pulp, add it to the meat mixture and mix well. Check the seasoning. Fill the aubergine shells with the mixture, brush with beaten egg and cover with breadcrumbs. Cook in a preheated oven, 200°C (400°F), Gas Mark 6, for about 10 minutes until they are cooked and golden brown.

Serves 4

Tip: To scoop out the flesh from the aubergine, cut around the edge of the aubergine between the skin and pulp, leaving a narrow margin of flesh adhering to the skin. Make criss-cross cuts over the surface before scooping out the pulp.

far left: kofta curry
below: aubergine cutlets

Lamb-stuffed Peppers

4 large green and yellow peppers
2 tablespoons vegetable oil
250 g (8 oz) lean minced lamb
1 onion, finely chopped
50 g (2 oz) mushrooms, finely chopped
40 g (1½ oz) fresh breadcrumbs
1 teaspoon grated lemon rind
1 teaspoon lemon juice
2 tablespoons chopped parsley
2 tablespoons chopped blanched almonds
4 tablespoons natural yogurt
salt and freshly ground black pepper

Cut off the tops from the peppers and set aside. Scoop out the cores and seeds. Blanch the peppers and their tops in boiling salted water for 5 minutes. Remove and drain.

Heat the oil in a pan and cook the minced lamb over a moderate heat for 4–5 minutes, stirring, until browned. Remove and set aside.

Fry the onion and mushrooms for 3 minutes, stirring once or twice. Return the lamb to the pan and cook, uncovered, for 15 minutes, stirring often.

Remove from the heat, season to taste with salt and pepper and mix in the breadcrumbs, lemon rind, juice, parsley, almonds and yogurt.

Stand the peppers upright in a baking dish that just fits them. Fill them with the lamb mixture and cover with the lids. Pour about 5 cm (2 inches) of water into the dish, cover with foil and then bake in a preheated oven, 190°C (375°F), Gas Mark 5, for 50 minutes. Remove the foil 15 minutes before the end. Serve the peppers hot.

Serves 4

Mince-filled Peppers

4 green, yellow or red peppers
300 g (10 oz) lean minced beef
1 onion, chopped
50 g (2 oz) mushrooms, sliced
3 tomatoes, chopped
1 slice bread, toasted and cubed
¼ teaspoon Worcestershire sauce
salt and freshly ground black pepper

Cut off the tops of the peppers and set aside. Remove the cores and the seeds. Cook the peppers for 5 minutes in a large saucepan of boiling salted water. Drain and season inside with salt and pepper.

Put the minced beef and onion in a non-stick frying pan and dry-fry, stirring, until evenly browned. Stir in the remaining ingredients and add salt and pepper to taste.

Spoon the beef mixture into the peppers and replace the tops. Stand upright in a baking dish and bake in a preheated oven, 190°C (375°F), Gas Mark 5, for about 25 minutes.

Serves 4

Bobotie

500 g (1 lb) lean minced beef or lamb
1 onion, finely chopped
1 tablespoon oil
1 garlic clove, crushed
3 teaspoons curry powder
1 dessert apple, cored, peeled and chopped
50 g (2 oz) sultanas
1 tablespoon chutney
25 g (1 oz) wholemeal breadcrumbs
2 eggs
300 ml (½ pint) semi-skimmed milk
25 g (1 oz) flaked almonds
3 bay leaves
salt and freshly ground black pepper

Put the minced beef or lamb into a large saucepan with the onion and oil. Cook over a moderate heat until the meat is browned and crumbly. Drain off any excess fat.

Add the garlic, curry powder and apple and cook for 2 minutes, stirring. Add the sultanas, chutney, breadcrumbs and seasoning. Turn into a greased ovenproof dish.

Beat together the eggs and milk and pour over the meat mixture. Scatter over the almonds and place the bay leaves on top. Bake in a preheated oven, 180°C (350°F), Gas Mark 4, for 45 minutes until set and golden on top. Serve immediately.

Serves 4

right: lamb-stuffed peppers

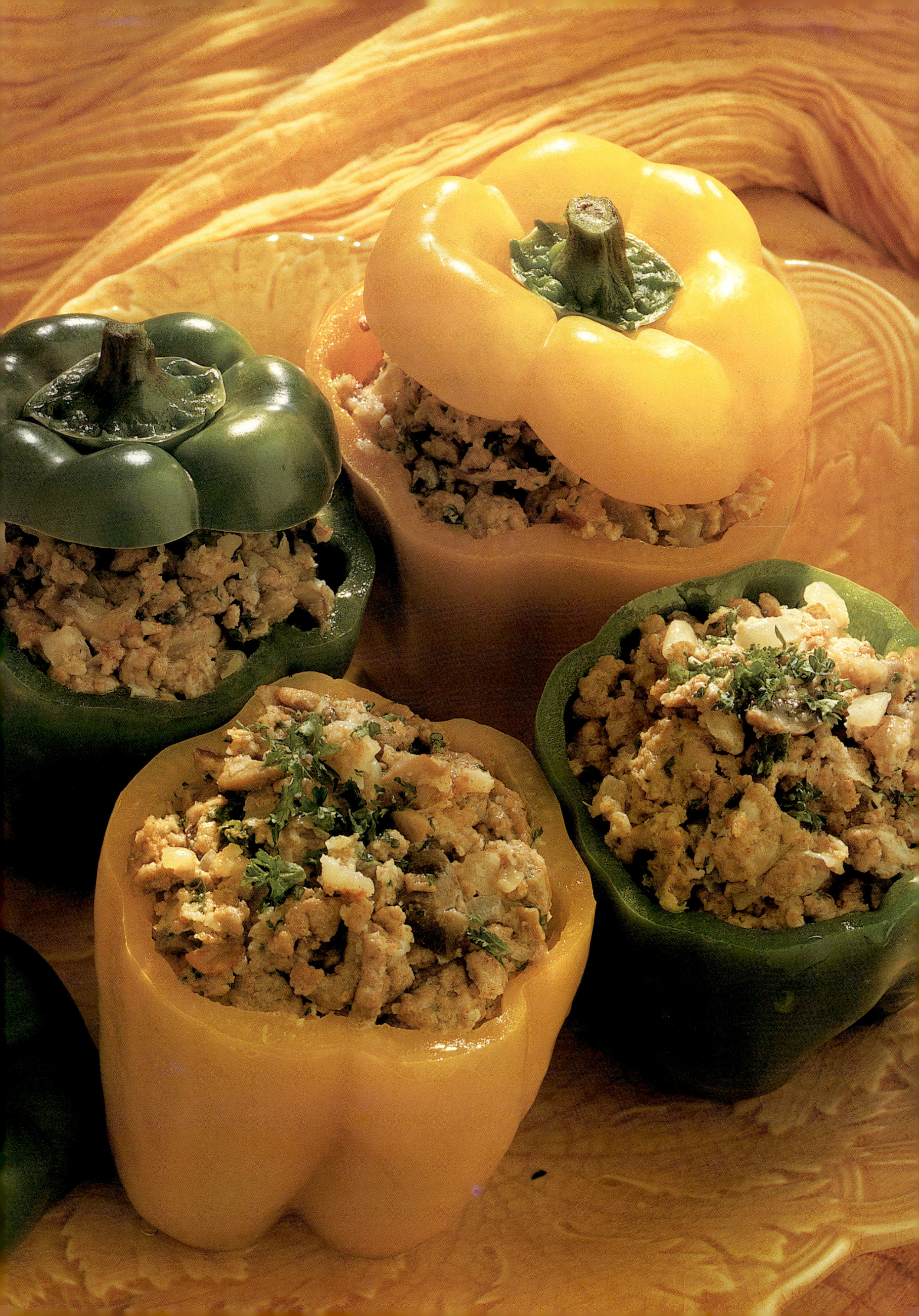

Shepherd's Oatmeal and Lamb Pie

Oats make a good high-fibre 'extender' for minced meats and give this dish an unusual nutty flavour.

500 g (1 lb) lean minced lamb
1 onion, thinly sliced
2 celery sticks, thinly sliced
5 tablespoons rolled oats
150 ml (¼ pint) lamb or beef stock
1 tablespoon tomato purée
750 g (1½ lb) potatoes, thinly sliced
1 tablespoon soya or sunflower oil
salt and pepper
chopped parsley, to garnish

In a large non-stick pan, fry the minced lamb without any added fat until it is evenly coloured. Add the onion and celery and cook for a further 2 minutes, stirring the mixture occasionally. Stir in the rolled oats, stock, tomato purée and salt and pepper. Cover the pan and simmer gently for 15 minutes.

Meanwhile, blanch the potato slices in a pan of boiling water for 30 seconds and then drain well. Transfer the lamb mixture to a wide 1.8 litre (3 pint) ovenproof dish. Arrange the potatoes attractively on top, brushing them with oil and sprinkling salt and pepper between the layers.

Cook the pie in a preheated oven, 200°C (400°F), Gas Mark 6, for 35–40 minutes until the potatoes are tender and golden brown. Serve immediately, garnished with some chopped parsley.

Serves 4

below: shepherd's oatmeal and lamb pie

Greek Shepherd's Pie

Here's a delicious shepherd's pie with a difference; the minced lamb is layered with sliced aubergine, tomatoes and potato before being baked in the oven. If wished, you could give this dish more of an authentic Greek flavour by grating some salty feta cheese on top.

1 large aubergine, sliced
1 tablespoon lemon juice
50 g (2 oz) butter
2 onions, thinly sliced
1 large potato, thinly sliced
500 g (1 lb) minced lamb
2 tomatoes, skinned and sliced
300 ml (½ pint) Béchamel Sauce (see page 26)
50 g (2 oz) grated cheese
salt and freshly ground black pepper

Arrange the sliced aubergine on a plate, sprinkle with a little salt and lemon juice and set aside to exude their bitter juices for 15 minutes. Rinse under running cold water, drain and dry on kitchen paper.

Heat the butter and gently fry the onions until softened. Remove from the pan and fry the aubergines until golden brown. Remove and set aside while you fry the potato, without breaking the slices. Remove and keep warm. Add the minced lamb and cook gently for a few minutes until lightly browned.

Place a layer of aubergine and onions in a casserole dish, and cover with some of the minced lamb and sliced tomatoes. Top with a little béchamel sauce, season well with salt and pepper and cover with the potato slices. Continue layering up the aubergine and onions, lamb and tomatoes in this way, finishing with a layer of sauce.

Sprinkle with grated cheese and cook the shepherd's pie, uncovered, in a preheated oven, 180°C (350°F), Gas Mark 4, for 45 minutes until golden brown and bubbling. Serve immediately while piping hot with green vegetables or salad.

Serves 4–6

Tamale Pie

1 tablespoon vegetable oil
375 g (12 oz) lean minced beef
1 onion, chopped
1 tablespoon chilli seasoning
1 teaspoon ground cumin
½ teaspoon salt (or to taste)
175 g (6 oz) can sweetcorn, drained
175 g (6 oz) can Italian peeled plum tomatoes, drained and coarsely chopped
1 green pepper, cored, deseeded and chopped
1 garlic clove, crushed (optional)
Topping:
125 g (4 oz) coarse yellow cornmeal
1 tablespoon plain flour
1 tablespoon caster sugar
1½ teaspoons baking powder
pinch of salt
50 ml (2 fl oz) milk
1 egg
15 g (½ oz) butter, melted

Heat the oil in a heavy frying pan and gently fry the meat until browned. Remove with a slotted spoon. Add the onion and cook until soft but not brown.

Remove the onion and fry the spices in the remaining oil, stirring, for 2 minutes. Return the meat and onion mixture to the pan with the salt, sweetcorn, tomatoes, green pepper and garlic (if using), and simmer for about 10 minutes. If it is too dry, add about 50–75 ml (2–3 fl oz) water. Check the seasoning, then turn into an oiled, shallow baking dish.

Sift the cornmeal, flour, sugar, baking powder and salt together. Beat the milk and egg together and stir – do not beat – into the cornmeal mixture. Add the melted butter and stir once or twice.

Spoon the cornmeal topping evenly over the meat. Bake the pie in a preheated oven, 200°C (400°F), Gas Mark 6, for about 25 minutes or until the cornmeal layer is well risen and golden brown. Serve immediately while still hot.

Serves 4

Spicy Shepherd's Pie

1 tablespoon oil
1 onion, chopped
25 g (1 oz) plain flour
300 ml (½ pint) hot beef stock
500 g (1 lb) cooked lamb, minced
1 tablespoon Worcestershire sauce
pinch of grated nutmeg
good pinch of mild curry powder
250 g (8 oz) can baked beans in tomato sauce
500 g (1 lb) cooked potatoes, mashed
salt and freshly ground black pepper
sprigs of parsley, to garnish

Heat the oil and fry the onion for 5 minutes until softened. Stir in the flour and cook for 1 minute.

Remove the pan from the heat and stir in the hot beef stock and minced lamb before adding the Worcestershire sauce, nutmeg and curry powder. Season to taste with salt and pepper. Return the pan to the heat and bring to the boil, then reduce the heat and simmer for 20 minutes. Add the baked beans and cook for a further 5 minutes.

Transfer to a heated flameproof dish. Spread the mashed potatoes evenly over the spicy lamb mixture and fork a pattern on the surface.

Cook the shepherd's pie in a preheated oven, 180°C (350°F), Gas Mark 4, for about 15 minutes until golden brown. Serve hot, garnished with sprigs of parsley, and with vegetables such as buttered sprouts.

Serves 4

Country Beef and Potato Pie

The various permutations of the humble cottage pie are literally endless. In this version, the beef mixture is topped with mashed potatoes and sweet parsnips.

1 tablespoon vegetable oil
1 large onion, finely chopped
1 large celery stick, finely chopped
750 g (1½ lb) lean minced beef
1 tablespoon plain flour
2 tablespoons tomato purée
150 ml (¼ pint) brown ale or beer
1 bay leaf
salt and pepper

Vegetable topping:
500 g (1 lb) potatoes
250 g (8 oz) parsnips
3 tablespoons milk
40 g (1½ oz) butter

Heat the oil in a frying pan, add the onion and celery and fry gently for about 5 minutes until soft but not coloured. Add the minced beef and cook, stirring, until brown.

Stir in the flour and cook for 1 minute. Add the tomato purée, ale or beer, and the bay leaf. Season with salt and pepper, and then bring to the boil. Reduce the heat, cover the pan and simmer gently for 30 minutes, stirring occasionally.

Meanwhile, prepare the vegetable topping. Cook the potatoes and parsnips in a large pan of boiling salted water until tender. Drain the vegetables, place in a large mixing

Index

Alabama chilli, 39
Aloo 'chops', 13
Angostura mince cobbler, 77
Ants climbing trees, 32
Aubergine cutlets, 85

Baja California guacamole hamburgers, 57
Beef and bean moussaka, 83
Beef and cabbage cobbler, 75
Beef and carrot mould, minced, 94
Beef gougère, 74
Beef, with lime rice, Mexican, 36
Beef, Ma Po's minced, 31
Beef noodle casserole, 29
Beef, okra and pepper mould, 76
Beef and olive pasties, 41
Beef and pasta supper, minced, 27
Beef patties, gingered, 79
Beef and peanut burgers, 56
Beef pizza, peppered, 49
Beef and potato clock flan, 47
Beef and potato pie, country, 90
Beef and raisin meatballs, 66
Beef with rice, paprika, 38
Beef samosas, 22
Beef and vegetable kheema, 82
Bobotie, 86
Burgers, beef and peanut, 56
Burgers, classic ham-, 60
Burgers, golden onion-, 58
Burgers, with guacamole, Mexican, 58
Burgers, mince and mushroom, 50

Cannelloni, 28
Cheesy-topped burgers, 54
Chicken swirls, 93
Chicken timbales tonnato, 92
Chilli calzone, 49
Chilli con carne, 37
Chillied meatballs, 68
Chillied meat koftas with mint, 50
Classic hamburgers, 60
Cobbler, Angostura mince, 77
Cobbler, beef and cabbage, 75
Cobbler, Texan, 78
Cocktail meatballs with barbecue dip, 17
Country beef and potato pie, 90
Courgette layer pie, 16
Curry, kofta, 84

Danish frikadeller, 60
Devilled meatballs, 64
Dolmas, 21
Dumplings, steamed Chinese, 12

Empanada, 44

Fried rice with pork and prawns, 35

Gingered beef patties, 79
Golden onionburgers, 58
Greek keftedes, 21
Greek shepherd's pie, 89
Guinness meat loaf, 69

Hamburgers, classic, 60
Hot-tossed noodles with spicy meat sauce, 30

Indian stuffed peppers, 91
Indonesian meatballs, 54
Italian porkballs, 68

Japanese pork balls with dipping sauce, 53

Kebab, mince, 20
Keftedes, Greek, 21
Kheema do pyaza, 78
Kofta curry, 84

Lamb with courgettes, tipsy, 80
Lamb with flageolet beans, 81
Lamb lasagne, 27
Lamb meatballs with apricot sauce, 62
Lamb, Middle Eastern, 33
Lamb and mint meatballs, 63
Lamb and Parmesan soufflé, minced, 18
Lamb rolls, minced, 42
Lamb samosas, 22
Lamb-stuffed peppers, 86
Lamb tart with apricots, spiced, 46
Lasagne,
  al forno, 26
  lamb, 27
Lentil mince with pasta, 24

Ma Po's minced beef, 31
Meatball minestrone, 14
Meat puffs, 40
Meatballs with apricot sauce, lamb, 62
Meatballs, beef and raisin, 67

Meatballs, chillied, 68
Meatballs, devilled, 64
Meatballs in horseradish sauce, 66
Meatballs, Indonesian, 54
Meatballs, lamb and mint, 63
Meatballs with mushroom sauce, tarragon, 56
Meatballs, Scandinavian, 60
Meatballs, skewered, 67
Meat loaf, 70
  Guinness, 69
  with spinach, 70
  turkey and broccoli, 72
  stuffed veal, 73
Mexicali pancakes, 48
Mexican beef with lime rice, 36
Mexican burgers with guacamole, 58
Mexican soup, 11
Middle Eastern lamb, 33
Mince-filled peppers, 86
Mince kebab, 20
Mince and mushroom burgers, 50
Minced beef and carrot mould, 94
Minced beef and pasta supper, 27
Minced lamb and Parmesan soufflé, 18
Minced lamb rolls, 42
Moussaka, 82
  beef and bean, 83
Mu shu pork pockets, 64

Noodles,
  casserole, beef, 29
  with spicy meat sauce, hot-tossed, 30

Omelette, Thai stuffed, 19

Pancakes, Mexicali, 48
Paprika beef with rice, 38
Pasta,
  lentil mince with, 24
  spaghetti alla Bolognese, 25
Pasties, beef and olive, 41
Pâté,
  pork and olive, 11
  rich pork, 10
Peppered beef pizza, 49
Pizza, peppered beef, 49
Porkballs with dipping sauce, Japanese, 53
Pork and olive pâté, 11
Pork parcels, Vietnamese, 8
Pork pie, raised, 45
Pork pockets, mu shu, 64

Pork, spiced beancurd with, 13
Pork, sweet and sour, 9
Pork terrine, 11
Porky oatmeal sausages, 52

Ragu Bolognese sauce, 25
Raised pork pie, 45
Rice with pork and prawns, fried, 35
Rich pork pâté, 10
Risotto, 34

Samosas, 22
Sauce(s),
  béchamel, 26
  ragu Bolognese, 25
  snappy cheese, 58
Sausages, porky oatmeal, 52
Savoury plait, 42
Scandinavian meatballs, 60
Shepherd's oatmeal and lamb pie, 88
Skewered meatballs, 67
Sloppy Joes, 23
Snappy cheese sauce, 58
Soup(s),
  meatball minestrone, 14
  Mexican, 11
Spaghetti alla Bolognese, 25
Spanish mince, 95
Spiced beancurd with pork, 13
Spiced lamb tart with apricots, 46
Spicy shepherd's pie, 90
Steak tartare, 17
Steamed Chinese dumplings, 12
Stuffed mushrooms, 17
Stuffed veal loaf, 73
Swedish meat cakes, 52
Sweet and sour minced pork, 9

Tacos, 14
Tamale pie, 89
Tarragon meatballs with mushroom sauce, 56
Texan cobbler, 78
Thai stuffed omelette, 19
Tipsy lamb with courgettes, 80
Tourtière, 43
Turkey and broccoli loaf, 72
Turkey roll en croûte, 94

Veal and apple pasties with walnuts, 46
Veal with chilli, 32
Veal and rosemary frikadeller, 59
Vietnamese pork parcels, 8

On a lightly floured surface, roll out the pastry into an oblong shape large enough to enclose the turkey roll with about 5 cm (2 inches) to spare down one long side. Put the turkey roll on the pastry, fold the opposite side over and trim off the excess, then press the join to seal it. Fold the ends over to enclose the filling completely, brushing with beaten egg where necessary and trimming off any excess pastry. Place the roll, seam-side down, on a greased baking tray.

Reroll the pastry trimmings and cut out as many leaves as you can. Brush with beaten egg and press on to the roll in a herringbone pattern. Glaze with beaten egg and bake in a preheated oven, 200°C (400°F) Gas Mark 6, for 1 hour, or until the pastry is well puffed up and golden brown. Serve immediately.

Serves 4-6

Spanish Mince

1 onion, thinly sliced
2 tablespoons oil
2 garlic cloves, crushed
550 g (1 lb 2 oz) minced beef
2 dessert apples, cored and grated
50 g (2 oz) raisins
300 ml (½ pint) beef stock
75 g (3 oz) stuffed olives, thickly sliced
coarsely grated rind of 1 orange
salt and pepper

Fry the onion in the oil in a frying pan for 2 minutes. Add the garlic and minced beef and cook gently, stirring occasionally, until browned. Stir in the apple, raisins and stock. Cover and simmer for 20 minutes.

Stir in the olives and orange rind and season to taste with salt and pepper. Simmer gently for a further 10 minutes. Serve with crusty bread and a green salad.

Serves 4

---

far left: minced beef and carrot mould
above: Spanish mince

Minced Beef and Carrot Mould

An economical meal for the family. If you're short of time, grate all the carrots instead of slicing those for the garnish.

250 g (8 oz) carrots
oil, for brushing
500 g (1 lb) lean minced beef
1 onion, finely chopped
50 g (2 oz) wholemeal breadcrumbs
1 tablespoon Worcestershire sauce
3 tablespoons tomato ketchup
1 egg, beaten
salt and pepper
sprigs of parsley, to garnish

Lightly oil a 1.2 litre (2 pint) ovenproof pudding basin. Thinly slice 1 carrot and grate the others coarsely. Arrange the slices of carrot over the base of the oiled basin.

In a bowl, combine the grated carrot with the minced beef, onion, breadcrumbs, Worcestershire sauce, ketchup and beaten egg and mix together evenly. Season with some salt and pepper.

Pack the mixture into the oiled pudding basin, taking care not to dislodge the carrot slices, and press it down firmly. Cover the basin with kitchen foil.

Bake the mould in a preheated oven, 180°C (350°F), Gas Mark 4, for about 1 hour or until the juices run clear. Cool for a few minutes, then turn out on to a serving plate. Serve garnished with parsley sprigs.

Serves 4

Turkey Roll en Croûte

250 g (8 oz) cream cheese with garlic and herbs
1 kg (2 lb) minced turkey
125 g (4 oz) fresh breadcrumbs
1 egg, beaten
400 g (13 oz) puff pastry, defrosted if frozen
salt and pepper
beaten egg, to glaze

Shape the cream cheese into a roll and leave to chill. Mix the turkey with the breadcrumbs, season with salt and pepper and mix in the beaten egg. Shape the turkey mixture evenly around the cream cheese roll to enclose it completely, including the ends. Chill while you roll out the pastry.

and softer. This will take some time but the dough must be smooth and pliable before you roll it out. Roll out the dough into a large rectangle measuring about 25 x 42 cm (10 x 17 inches).

Mix the minced chicken with the breadcrumbs, the beaten egg and the basil. Season to taste with salt and pepper.

Brush the pasta all over with some of the remaining beaten egg, then spread the chicken mixture over it, leaving a border all the way round. Roll up from the long end, brushing more egg over the pasta as you roll it up. Make sure the end is well brushed with beaten egg and press it down firmly. Trim off the very end of the roll, then use a sharp serrated knife to cut the rest into 16 slices.

Bring a large pan of salted water to the boil and add a little oil. Cook the pasta swirls by lowering them gently into the water. You may have to do this in batches. Bring back to the boil and boil for 1 minute. Use a slotted spoon to lift the swirls from the water, then put them in a large ovenproof dish.

Stir the tomato purée in to the chicken stock and add enough wine to make 600 ml (1 pint). Add a little garlic salt and pour the liquid over the pasta swirls. Cover with foil and bake in a preheated oven, 180°C (350°F) Gas Mark 4, for 1 hour.

Sprinkle the cheese over the swirls and cook under a hot grill until golden. Serve immediately with a green salad.

Serves 4

Chicken Timbales Tonnato

Most people are familiar with veal tonnato, a regional Italian dish, but in this variation, chicken is used instead and the mixture is cooked in little ramekins. If smaller moulds were used, this dish could be served as a starter.

750 g (1½ lb) minced chicken
75 g (3 oz) fresh white breadcrumbs
1 egg, beaten
grated rind of 1 small lemon
2 tablespoons double cream
butter, for dotting
salt and pepper
mixed vegetables, to serve
Sauce:
200 g (7 oz) can tuna in oil
1 garlic clove, crushed
2 tablespoons lemon juice
150 ml (¼ pint) mayonnaise
To garnish:
cucumber
4 lemon twists

Mix the minced chicken with the breadcrumbs, beaten egg and lemon rind and season lightly with salt and pepper. Stir in the cream.

Line the bases of 4 large or 8 small ramekin dishes with some greaseproof paper and make sure they are well greased. Divide the chicken mixture between the dishes and dot the top of each one with a little butter. Put a small piece of greaseproof paper on top of each and stand the ramekins in a large roasting tin. Pour boiling water into the tin around the ramekins to come halfway up the sides of the outer tin. Bake the timbales in a preheated oven, 180°C (350°F) Gas Mark 4, for 45 minutes.

For the sauce, mash the tuna with the oil from the can, the garlic and lemon juice or, alternatively, blend in a liquidizer or food processor until well mixed and smooth. Stir in the mayonnaise and season to taste with salt and pepper. Chill in the refrigerator for at least 30 minutes.

For the garnish, cut 2 pieces of cucumber in half lengthways, then cut each piece into long thin slices, leaving them attached at one end. Place the cucumber pieces in ice-cold water to open out.

Turn out the cooked timbales and remove the greaseproof paper. Put 2 timbales on each serving plate (or one if you are serving eight people as a first course) and add a piece of cucumber to each portion, opening out the slices like a fan. Add a twist of lemon and serve, handing the sauce separately. Serve with broccoli, mangetout, French beans or courgettes and potatoes.

Serves 4

Chicken Swirls

125 g (4 oz) strong plain flour
1 large egg
1½ tablespoons olive oil
1–2 beaten eggs, for sealing
50 g (2 oz) Gruyère cheese, grated
4 tablespoons tomato purée
300 ml (½ pint) chicken stock
about 300 ml (½ pint) full-bodied red wine
garlic salt
salt and pepper
green salad, to serve
Filling:
500 g (1 lb) minced chicken
50 g (2 oz) fresh breadcrumbs
1 egg, beaten
2 tablespoons chopped basil

Make the pasta dough. Sift the flour into a bowl and add a generous pinch of salt. Make a well in the centre and break in the egg. Pour the oil over the egg, and then beat it well with a wooden spoon.

Gradually work in the flour, pounding the mixture with the wooden spoon to help it bind together. The mixture will appear quite stiff. When it starts to clump together, scrape all the bits off the wooden spoon and use your hands to knead it into a dough.

Turn the dough out on to a lightly floured work surface and knead it until it is smooth and

far right: chicken timbales tonnato, chicken swirls

bowl, and mash them together smoothly. Beat in the milk with one-third of the butter and seasoning to taste, and mix well.

Turn the mince mixture into a shallow 1.5 litre (2½ pint) ovenproof dish. Pipe over or cover with the vegetable topping and then mark decoratively with a fork. Melt the remaining butter and brush over the top of the pie. Bake in a preheated oven, 180°C (350°F), Gas Mark 4, for 45 minutes or until the topping is golden brown.

Serves 4–6

left: country beef and potato pie
below: Indian stuffed peppers

Indian Stuffed Peppers

5 tablespoons oil
1 onion, finely chopped
2 teaspoons ground coriander
1 teaspoon ground cumin
½ teaspoon chilli powder
375 g (12 oz) lean minced beef
3 tablespoons long-grain rice
4 large green or red peppers, cut in half lengthways, cored and deseeded
425 g (14 oz) can tomatoes with juice
salt and freshly ground black pepper

Heat 3 tablespoons of the oil in a pan. Add the onion and fry until golden. Stir in the spices and cook for 2 minutes. Add the minced beef and fry, stirring, until browned. Add the rice and salt to taste and cook for 2 more minutes. Remove from the heat and leave to cool, then fill the pepper shells with the mixture.

Heat the remaining oil in a roasting pan just large enough to hold the peppers. Add the stuffed peppers and pour a little of the canned tomato juice over each pepper. Spoon the remaining juice and tomatoes into the pan around the peppers, seasoning to taste with salt and pepper. Bring to simmering point, cover with foil and cook in a preheated oven, 180°C (350°F), Gas Mark 4, for about 25 minutes until the rice is tender.

Serves 4